WALKING THE CAMMINO MATERANO

THREE LONG-DISTANCE ROUTES IN ITALY'S PUGLIA AND BASILICATA REGIONS TO MATERA

by Gillian Price

CICERONE

JUNIPER HOUSE, MURLEY MOSS,
OXENHOLME ROAD, KENDAL, CUMBRIA LA9 7RL
www.cicerone.co.uk

© Gillian Price 2025
First edition 2025
ISBN: 978 1 78631 260 0
eISBN: 978 1 78765 224 8

Printed in Czechia on responsibly sourced paper on behalf of Latitude Press Ltd.
A catalogue record for this book is available from the British Library.
Photographs are by Gillian Price, with additional images from Cammino
Materano (CM), Jonathan and Lesley Williams (JL) and Laura Stevenson (LS).

Route mapping by Lovell Johns www.lovelljohns.com
Contains OpenStreetMap.org data © OpenStreetMap contribu-
tors, CC-BY-SA. NASA relief data courtesy of ESRI
Cicerone's EU representative for GPSR compliance is Easy Access System Europe,
Mustamäe tee 50, 10621 Tallinn, Estonia. Email gpsr.requests@easproject.com

To my dear Nick, who else

Updates to this guide

While every effort is made by our authors to ensure the accuracy of guide-
books as they go to print, changes can occur during the lifetime of an edition. Any updates that we know of for this guide will be on the Cicerone
website (www.cicerone.co.uk/1260/updates), so please check before
planning your trip. We also advise that you check information about such
things as transport, accommodation and shops locally. Even rights of way
can be altered over time.

The route maps in this guide are derived from publicly available data,
databases and crowd-sourced data. As such they have not been through
the detailed checking procedures that would generally be applied to a
published map from an official mapping agency, although naturally we
have reviewed them closely in the light of local knowledge as part of the
preparation of this guide.

We are always grateful for information about any discrepancies
between a guidebook and the facts on the ground, sent by email to
updates@cicerone.co.uk.

Register your book: To sign up to receive free updates, special offers
and GPX files where available, create a Cicerone account and register your
purchase via the 'My Account' tab at www.cicerone.co.uk.

Front cover: Gravina in Puglia and its marvellous bridge (VP Stage 4)

CONTENTS

Acknowledgements

A very special mention for Colleen and Laura, my treasured support drivers armed with great patience and navigation skills. Laura also scouted the sunblasted Via Ellenica, while champions Jonathan and Lesley dashed over to recheck the Via Peuceta, which resulted in them learning the word *fango* (Italian for 'mud'); some of their precious notes and photos are in this book.

But I have a host more people to thank. This guidebook wouldn't have been possible without the inspiration and generous help of the community of volunteers who believe in the Cammino Materano project, tirelessly maintaining paths and waymarking, and providing info and inspirational assistance and company to walkers – and writers! *Grazie di cuore* (heartfelt thanks) to Antonio C, Antonio M, Claudio, Concetta, Francesco, Gianluca, Gianni, Giovanni, Giulio, Leo G, Leo P, Liliana, Lorenzo, Marilena, Mino, Nadia, Nunzio, Paolo, Rosa – really sorry if I've left anyone out! And how could I forget the accommodation hosts with their warm hospitality and delightful premises, and the talented village brass bands with their smile-inducing music.

Along the way I was also lucky to make the acquaintance of olive farmers, grape growers, winemakers, priests, village inhabitants, café tenders, master bakers and mozzarella makers who enriched me with their accounts of life and supplied me with coffee, bread, music, almonds, figs, *fave con cicoria*, cheese, *taralli* and every imaginable type of focaccia.

And I wouldn't dream of glossing over key players and encouragers Sandy, Angelo and Joe, not to mention meticulous editor Pat Dunn, and the talented Cicerone team who put the book together.

ROUTE ABBREVIATIONS

Throughout this Cammino Materano (CM) guide, the following abbreviations are used to refer to the three routes:

VE	Via Ellenica
VL	Via Lucana
VP	Via Peuceta

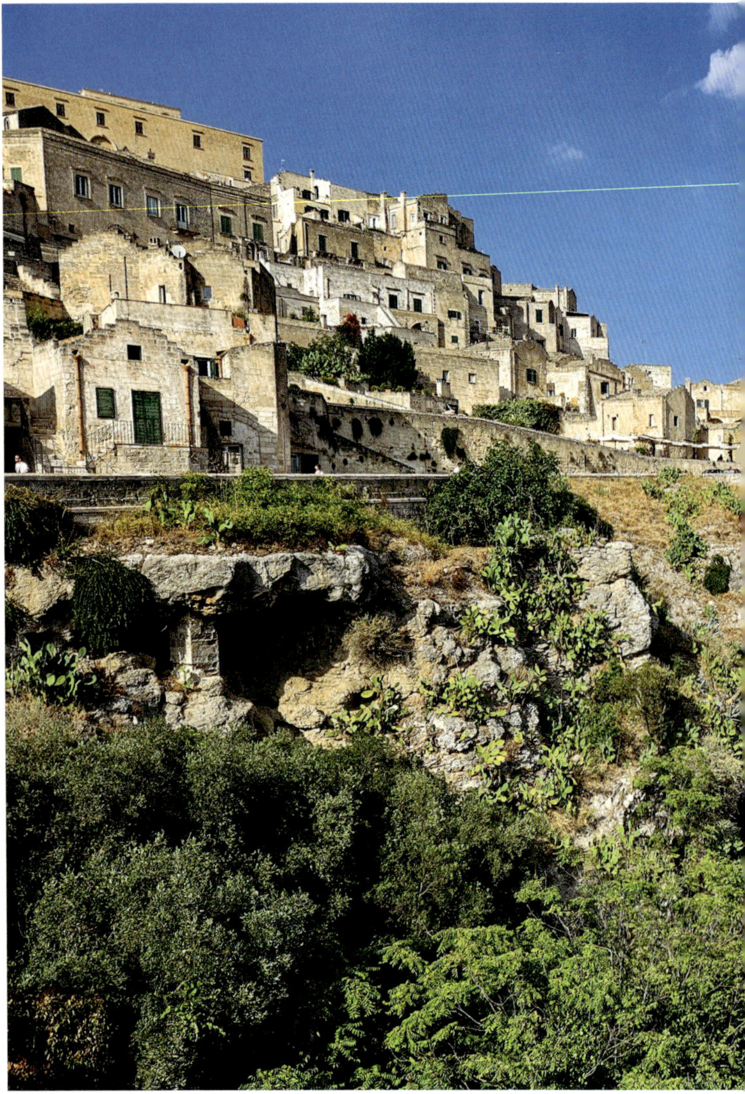

Matera and its gravina (VP Stage 7)

ROUTE SUMMARY TABLES

Stage	Start	Finish	
VIA PEUCETA			
1	Bari	Bitetto	
2	Bitetto	Cassano delle Murge	
3	Cassano delle Murge	Santeramo in Colle	
4	Santeramo in Colle	Altamura	
5	Altamura	Gravina in Puglia	
6	Gravina in Puglia	Santuario di Picciano	
7	Santuario di Picciano	Matera	
Total			
VIA ELLENICA			
1	Brindisi	San Vito dei Normanni	
2	San Vito dei Normanni	Carovigno	
3	Carovigno	Ostuni	
4	Ostuni	Cisternino	
5	Cisternino	Locorotondo	
6	Locorotondo	Alberobello	
7	Alberobello	Martina Franca	
8	Martina Franca	Crispiano	
9	Crispiano	Massafra	
10	Massafra	Mottola	
11	Mottola	Castellaneta	
12	Castellaneta	Laterza	
13	Laterza	Ginosa	
14	Ginosa	Matera	
Total			
VIA LUCANA			
1	Tricarico	Grassano	
2	Grassano	Grottole	
3	Grottole	Miglionico	
4	Miglionico	Pomarico	
5	Pomarico	Montescaglioso	
6	Montescaglioso	Matera	
Total			

Time	Distance	Ascent	Descent	Page
4hr 15min	17km	160m	40m	45
6hr 15min	25km	300m	100m	50
5hr 45min	22.5km	420m	240m	54
5hr 45min	23km	290m	300m	58
5hr	20km	200m	340m	62
7hr 30min	30.3km	720m	620m	65
7hr 30min	29.7km	530m	570m	69
42hr	**167.5km**	**2620m**	**2210m**	
6hr	27.8km	165m	60m	80
3hr	9.8km	90m	30m	84
5hr	20.3km	290m	250m	87
5hr	19.8km	540m	350m	90
4hr 30min	16km	200m	190m	94
6hr	23km	340m	315m	97
5hr	18km	290m	270m	100
8hr	27.4km	390m	585m	104
5hr	18km	165m	325m	108
6hr 30min	23km	580m	315m	111
5hr	17.5km	340m	475m	114
7hr	24km	635m	535m	118
4hr 30min	16km	255m	345m	122
6hr 30min	27km	535m	380m	125
77hr	**287.6km**	**4865m**	**4425m**	
5hr	20.5km	720m	865m	134
6hr	19.8km	710m	770m	138
5hr	17km	445m	450m	141
4hr 30min	16km	215m	255m	144
6hr 30min	22.8km	405m	470m	148
5hr 30min	18.5km	435m	395m	152
32hr 30min	**114.6km**	**2930m**	**3205m**	

9

WALKING THE CAMMINO MATERANO

STAGE FACILITIES PLANNERS

Stage	Place	Cumulative stage time	Cumulative stage distance
VIA PEUCETA			
1	**Bari**	–	–
1	Lidl supermarket	1hr	4km
1	Shopping centre	1hr 35min	6.5km
1	*Balsignano*	*depart main route at 3hr/12km; +5min/500m*	
1	**Bitetto**	**4hr 15min**	**17km**
2	**Cassano delle Murge**	**6hr 15min**	**25km**
3	Agriturismo Battista	50min	3km
3	Masseria Ruotolo	1hr 25min	5.5km
3	Agriturismo Amicizia	2hr	7.5km
3	Parco dei Briganti	3hr 10min	12km
3	Masseria Galietti	5hr 10min	19km
3	**Santeramo in Colle**	**5hr 45min**	**22.5km**
4	Masseria Scalera	3hr	12.5km
4	**Altamura**	**5hr 45min**	**23km**
5	**Gravina in Puglia**	**5hr**	**20km**
6	*Masseria Santa Maria*	*depart main route at 5hr 30min/20.2km; +35min/3.5km*	
6	**Santuario di Picciano**	**7hr 30min**	**30.3km**
6	*Masseria La Fiorita*	*pickup from Santuario di Picciano*	
7	Petrol station	4hr 30min	18.5km
7	**Matera**	**7hr 30min**	**29.7km**

Stage	Place	Cumulative stage time	Cumulative stage distance
VIA ELLENICA			
1	**Brindisi**	–	–
1	**San Vito dei Normanni**	**6hr**	**27.8km**
2	**Carovigno**	**3hr**	**9.8km**
3	B&B La Vigna	1hr 15min	5.5km
3	**Ostuni**	**5hr**	**20.3km**

Legend:
- ▲ accommodation available
- 🍴 refreshments
- shop
- ATM
- ⊕ pharmacy
- 𝒊 information
- ◼ train station
- ◼ bus service

Facility							
accommodation	refreshments	shop	ATM	pharmacy	information	train station	bus service
▲	🍴	shop	ATM	⊕	𝒊	◼	◼
		shop					
	🍴	shop					
	🍴						
▲	🍴	shop	ATM	⊕		◼	◼
▲	🍴	shop	ATM	⊕	𝒊		◼
▲	🍴						
▲	🍴						
▲	🍴						
	🍴						
▲							
▲	🍴	shop	ATM	⊕	𝒊	◼	◼
	🍴						
▲	🍴	shop	ATM	⊕	𝒊	◼	◼
▲	🍴	shop	ATM	⊕	𝒊	◼	◼
▲	🍴						
▲	🍴						
	🍴						
▲	🍴	shop	ATM	⊕	𝒊	◼	◼

Facility							
accommodation	refreshments	shop	ATM	pharmacy	information	train station	bus service
▲	🍴	shop	ATM	⊕	𝒊	◼	◼
▲	🍴	shop	ATM	⊕	𝒊		◼
▲	🍴	shop	ATM	⊕	𝒊		◼
▲							
▲	🍴	shop	ATM	⊕	𝒊		◼

Stage	Place	Cumulative stage time	Cumulative stage distance
4	**Cisternino**	**5hr**	**19.8km**
5	*café*	*depart main route at 2hr 15min/8km; +5min/100m*	
5	**Locorotondo**	**4hr 30min**	**16km**
6	*Coreggia*	*depart main route at 4hr 45min/17.7km; +5min/400m*	
6	**Alberobello**	**6hr**	**23km**
7	**Martina Franca**	**5hr**	**18km**
8	Masseria Querciulo	4hr	14km
8	Foresteria Bosco delle Pianelle	6hr 30min	22km
8	**Crispiano**	**8hr**	**27.4km**
9	Masseria Amastuola	3hr 20min	11.2km
9	**Massafra**	**5hr**	**18km**
10	**Mottola**	**6hr 30min**	**23km**
11	Palagianello	3hr	10.6km
11	**Castellaneta**	**5hr**	**17.5km**
12	**Laterza**	**7hr**	**24km**
13	**Ginosa**	**4hr 30min**	**16km**
14	**Matera**	**6hr 30min**	**27km**

Stage	Place	Cumulative stage time	Cumulative stage distance
VIA LUCANA			
1	**Tricarico**	–	–
1	*Ristoro dell'Anno Santo*	*depart main route at 2hr 45min/14km; +20min/800m*	
1	**Grassano**	**5hr**	**20.5km**
2	**Grottole**	**6hr**	**19.8km**
3	**Miglionico**	**5hr**	**17km**
4	**Pomarico**	**4hr 30min**	**16km**
5	villaggio rurale	3hr 15min	11km
5	Agriturismo L'Orto di Lucania	4hr 30min	16.7km
5	**Montescaglioso**	**6hr 30min**	**22.8km**
6	**Matera**	**5hr 30min**	**18.5km**

Facility							
🔺	🍴	🔵	ATM	⊕		🟥	🔵
	🍴						
🔺	🍴	🔵	ATM	⊕	ℹ	🟥	🔵
🔺	🍴	🔵					
🔺	🍴	🔵	ATM	⊕	ℹ	🟥	🔵
🔺	🍴	🔵	ATM	⊕	ℹ	🟥	🔵
	🍴						
🔺							
🔺	🍴	🔵	ATM	⊕			🔵
🔺	🍴						
🔺	🍴	🔵	ATM	⊕	ℹ	🟥	🔵
🔺	🍴	🔵	ATM	⊕	ℹ		🔵
	🍴	🔵	ATM	⊕		🟥	🔵
🔺	🍴	🔵	ATM	⊕	ℹ	🟥	🔵
🔺	🍴	🔵	ATM	⊕	ℹ		🔵
🔺	🍴	🔵	ATM	⊕			🔵
🔺	🍴	🔵	ATM	⊕	ℹ	🟥	🔵

Facility							
🔺	🍴	🔵	ATM	⊕			🔵
	🍴						
🔺	🍴	🔵	ATM	⊕			🔵
🔺	🍴	🔵	ATM	⊕			🔵
🔺	🍴	🔵	ATM	⊕	ℹ		🔵
🔺	🍴	🔵	ATM	⊕			🔵
	🍴						
🔺	🍴						
🔺	🍴	🔵	ATM	⊕	ℹ		🔵
🔺	🍴	🔵	ATM	⊕	ℹ	🟥	🔵

Matera by night

FOREWORDS

Interest in slow sustainable tourism has grown exponentially over recent years as travellers from all over the world seek authentic experiences beyond popular tourist destinations. As cultural itineraries, *cammino* routes satisfy this as they embrace the history, nature and anthropology of the lands they traverse.

The Cammino Materano is one of these special routes: a journey through the throbbing heart of Puglia and Basilicata, through the Murgia and the Terra delle Gravine regions, concluding at the remarkable UNESCO World Heritage city of Matera, symbol of the capacity to combine history and innovation. This cammino follows ancient routes trodden over centuries by pilgrims, traders and wayfarers; modern-day walkers get the opportunity to rediscover the meaning of journeying, inclusive of encounters, reflection and connection with the land.

The south of Italy offers visitors from overseas experiences that are both unique and unrepeatable. They will find genuine hospitality in welcoming villages with communities keen to share their traditions. They can immerse themselves in marvellous landscapes ranging from the rolling hills of the Murgia to rocky plateaus, atmospheric canyons and centuries-old woodlands. Every step on the Cammino Materano is a journey in time: from ancient Roman ways to cliffside sanctuaries, Norman castles to Baroque palaces, each and every stone narrates a rich fascinating past.

However, the Cammino Materano is not only a cultural experience: it is also a journey into the flavours and scents of a generous land where the local cuisine and its simple genuine ingredients are part and parcel of the route. Wayfarers will have the pleasure of savouring the olives of Bitetto, the bread from Altamura and Laterza, the *capocollo* of Martina Franca, extra virgin olive oil, traditional cheeses and dishes that recount centuries of Mediterranean influence.

This guide was written for an international readership and aims to be inspirational as well as practical for intending walkers. As they embark on the routes, walkers will discover that southern Italy is not merely a destination, but a state of mind, an area where time has a different rhythm, infused with beauty, authenticity and memorable encounters.

We extend an invitation to all those desirous of a profound meaningful travel experience to set out on the trail. The Cammino Materano is waiting to be discovered, step by step.

Aldo Patruno,
Director of the Department of Tourism,
Economy of Culture and Territorial
Appreciation, Regione Puglia

REGIONE PUGLIA

PACT
Polo
Arti Cultura Turismo
Regione Puglia

Lovely country lane on the Via Ellenica Stage 4 (photo: Laura Stevenson)

The Cammino Materano is not just a cammino, it's more than that. It's a social project inspired by commitment, participation and determination. It's probably not that easy for a foreigner to comprehend its contradictions: how marvellous and fascinating it is, but what a difficult place it is to live in due to the shortage of work, services and prospects. The inhabitants have been leaving for decades, above all young people who go to make a new life elsewhere. Recent studies show that the south of Italy will have lost a good 3.6 million inhabitants by the year 2050, a considerable decline in population along with economic, social and cultural impoverishment.

Exactly 10 years ago, in 2015, after experiences overseas and during a full-blown economic crisis, we decided to return and attempt to create something that would help change the future of the land where we were born. At that time there were only a handful of *cammini* in Italy, and nothing of the sort in the south. We were unemployed and had no money to invest, but what we could count on was our resolve along with expertise as archaeologists and walking guides, not to mention experience on the Camino de Santiago, the French *Grandes Randonnées*, and treks in India and South East Asia.

So it was that we began to plan the Via Peuceta, one step at a time. We founded an association and began to organise events (walks and cammini) to cover expenses (petrol for site checks, signposting, an accountant, website) and the construction of a walkers' route, as well as meetings with local communities to explain the advantages of slow tourism. At the time, local institutions were not at all interested.

Matters then took a surprising turn: our events were attracting many followers, and the first *via*, the Peuceta, was opened. A large number of wayfarers – both Italian and international – began to walk the paths of Puglia and Basilicata, heading for Matera. Moreover, people in Puglia and the Lucania district of Basilicata, enthusiastic foot travellers like us, became cammino volunteers. Then we saw the first 'cammino houses', and bit by bit a network of accommodation and eateries was constructed in the end-of-stage villages. A sizeable community was mobilised to support and participate in this ongoing collective project.

Since then, the Cammino Materano has become a solid reality. After the Via Peuceta, the Via Ellenica was opened in 2019, then the Via Lucana in 2023. The Via Sveva, Via Jonica and Via Dauna are due to be opened in the coming years. The Cammino has been recognised as a project of national interest by the Italian Ministry for Tourism and the Puglia Region, which has decided to support this guidebook so as to attract visitors from all over the world. A new generation of council administrators is more receptive to the theme of slow tourism, and the Cammino Materano is often at the forefront of this for its participative model of 'community committees'; it has become a seed for change.

Once you've read this guidebook, whether you decide to undertake one via or all of them, you'll realise that they're the outcome of ideas that have taken time and effort to be transformed into reality, radical choices carried through with determination, aiming to provide opportunities for ourselves and the whole of southern Italy. Your credential won't just be a simple piece of paper, but will testify to your active participation in accompanying southern Italy towards a sustainable future; this is the only possible way to preserve the marvels of this area – marvels of nature, culture and people that are revealed exclusively to those who explore it on foot.

Buon cammino and happy encounters.

Lorenzo Lozito and Claudio Focarazzo,
Cammino Materano ETS (Management body of Cammino Materano)

With the supervision of Angelofabio Attolico, Regione Puglia Technical
Coordinator of the Committee for Ways, Cultural Routes and Cycle Tourism

with the support of:

Narrow streets enter Bitetto (VP Stage 1)

Piazzetta
PORTAPIS

INTRODUCTION: THE CAMMINO MATERANO

The Via Peuceta crosses open fields (VP Stage 5; photo: CM)

The Cammino Materano (CM) is a memorable multi-faceted adventure with three long-distance routes that are key to discovering two magical yet little-heard-of regions of Italy: Puglia and Basilicata. A good month's worth of walking is described in this guide for visitors who are keen on exploring on foot.

Running between the southern Adriatic coast of Italy and the Ionian Sea are extensive low-lying plains planted with kilometre after kilometre of olives and grapevines, edged with prickly pear cactus. Lush doesn't come to mind at first. Arid and harsh at times, yes. And magnificent in its vastness, with lungfuls of space. Moving inland following the CM routes, the terrain becomes hillier, nourishing abundant seas of wheat – gorgeously green and flourishing in the months preceding late summer, when harvest brings palettes of yellows and gold. But there's more. Much more. Vast woods of Mediterranean oaks and pine thrive, then a mere 30km from the seafront, yawning canyons known as *gravine* (ravines) gash into immense limestone plateaus, dotted with ancient cave settlements.

The CM is a community project created by a group of people genuinely inspired to make a difference: to entice and invite tourists to visit their area in a sustainable way – on foot – and generate related work opportunities at a local level, thus encouraging their fellow citizens to make their lives and a living in the region without 'fleeing' to the north of Italy.

SAINT EULIGIO

Although the CM routes are not pilgrimages, they are of rich historical significance. However, since the majority of Europe's cammini are associated with a religious figure or a saint, the CM committee decided that a saint would fit in nicely here too. So they proceeded to invent one of their own – a complete fake: his name is Sant'Euligio (pronounced 'ay-oo-lee-gee-o') of Marbella.

As the legend goes, he was crossing the Alps and got caught out in a bad storm. A black sheep appeared and led him to a tree miraculously hung with juicy roast pork shanks, fortuitously close to a spring gushing life-saving cool beer! So it was that Sant'Euligio became the patron saint of pork shanks and beer – and of the CM.

If you decide to pay 'homage' to him, go to the Pecora Nera (black sheep) pub at Cassano delle Murge on the Via Peuceta, where his statue adorns the bar. You may even be lucky enough to witness the annual 'miracle' when he bursts out laughing – but that only happens on his feast day, 20 April.

Three distinct routes have been created and are up and running, with more in the long-term pipeline. The Via Peuceta (VP), Via Ellenica (VE) and Via Lucana (VL) are described in this guidebook, each traversing quite different landscapes with embedded history and culture, and all trekking towards an unforgettable conclusion at magical Matera, a UNESCO World Heritage Site. Along the way, they journey through Puglia and a corner of the Basilicata region, linking rural towns and villages where people have lived for centuries. Each has its unique character, topography, history, art treasures, bread, saints and festivities, not forgetting friendly inhabitants who extend a warm greeting to visitors. Go with an open mind and heart, consider yourself a privileged onlooker, don't rush, and find out for yourself. What better way to visit than on foot?

Santo Euligio da Malberra
protettore del meglio Stinco della terra

Sant'Euligio, the 'fake' patron saint of the Cammino Materano

MATERA

All the cammini lead to...Matera. Imagine a dramatically deep ravine with cliffside cavities – some of them dwellings, some stables, others chapels. And a full-scale town complete with churches and palaces 'growing' out of the rock. People have lived here since Palaeolithic times. Matera's historic heart, a sprawling rock settlement referred to as the Sassi, a maze of tiny alleys and narrow streets, was once home to families dwelling in underground cavities transformed into simple houses, which they shared with their livestock. It hummed with life.

However, living conditions were primitive, with no sanitation or running water. In 1952 the Italian government declared it the 'disgrace of Italy', bought the whole place, and moved the inhabitants lock, stock and barrel into modern houses in satellite settlements scattered around the countryside, with varying degrees of success. The Sassi district has since been consolidated and renovated, and around a thousand Materesi have trickled back to make their homes there again; that said, a good number of the buildings are now tourism related.

Matera earned UNESCO World Heritage recognition in 1993 and was European Capital of Culture in 2019. Other claims to fame are as a film set for Mel Gibson's *The Passion of Christ* (2004) and the 2021 James Bond film *No Time to Die* (although the opening sequence of the latter was shot in nearby Gravina di Puglia).

Don't commit the unforgivable sin of rushing away as soon as your walk is over, but spend a couple of days absorbing the unique atmosphere. This extraordinary town begs to be visited slowly.

The three cammini are summarised below to help you make a choice and begin planning. Should all three sound irresistible, take extra holidays and do them all – easy decision! Time permitting, factor in rest days and in-depth visits. There's a wealth of places to explore: remarkable mazes of underground settlements, rock dwellings, canyons, churches, museums and farms.

A final note of encouragement: many visitors – male and female alike – walk on their own. However you go, rest assured that you'll come away from the CM with a list of new friends.

VIA PEUCETA – 7 DAYS, 167.5KM

Pronounced 'pay-oo-chetta', this route refers to the original name of the vast territory of Peucezia, after the pre-Roman tribe that inhabited it in the 7th–4th centuries BC.

Starting out from the historic seafront port of Bari, a whole week is spent heading inland through olive groves, wheat fields and woodland, and across a steppe-like plateau, with overnight stays in quiet villages and historic towns that are treasure troves of art and architecture. The walking is fairly strenuous but there are multiple highlights: the Romanesque cathedral at Bitetto, Altamura with its archaeological museum, the awesome ravine and underground rock dwellings at Gravina di Puglia, then the conclusion at magical Matera.

VIA ELLENICA – 14 DAYS, 287.6KM

Named after the Greeks (Hellenics) who colonised large tracts of Puglia's Adriatic coast in ancient times, this varied route sets out from the harbour of the strategic city of Brindisi. It heads west to wander along the Valle d'Itria, home to ancient olive trees, before entering the land of the *trulli*, curious traditional conical tiled huts. A string of fascinating bleached white villages are visited – Ostuni, Cisternino and Alberobello stand out.

The route then moves onto rugged rocky terrain sliced through by wild and wonderful canyons known locally as gravine; those near Laterza and Ginosa are particularly impressive. Man made his home in many of them, and scooped-out cave dwellings, stables and even frescoed chapels can still be admired in the cliff faces. Along the way are elegant towns such as Martina Franca, Massafra and Mottola on the lead-up to Matera.

VIA LUCANA – 6 DAYS, 114.6KM

The newest of the CM routes, the Via Lucana was inaugurated in 2023 and is wholly in Basilicata. Lucania was an ancient region that stretched from the Tyrrhenian Sea over to the Gulf of Taranto; the name is still used and also lives on in Amaro Lucano, a digestive liqueur.

Setting out from Tricarico, this route has more height gain and loss than the others but similarly spends day after peaceful day wandering over hills enjoying vast landscapes. Rural is the over-riding flavour, with wheat fields, olive groves and fruit trees. The Via Lucana links a succession of old villages and small towns set dramatically on windswept ridges once essential to their survival, with watchtowers and defensive walls to protect them from invaders. Today, their paved narrow streets and jumble of tightly packed houses with old tiled roofs are watched over by clouds of chattering jackdaws.

The Via Appia, the great ancient Roman military way linking Rome with Brindisi, ran through many of the valleys now visited by the Via Lucana.

Cammino Materano signpost

SHORTER AND LONGER COMBINATIONS

The routes are open to myriad variations to fit in with holiday needs. Thanks to easy access by public transport to almost every stage end, and the availability of GPX tracks, there's no reason walkers can't do their own thing and organise bespoke itineraries, change direction, and mix and match. Suggestions:

- **One week**: the Via Peuceta, the Via Lucana or a section of the Via Ellenica from Alberobello to Matera.
- **Two weeks**: the complete Via Ellenica from Brindisi to Matera, otherwise the Via Peuceta from Bari to Matera then continue to Tricarico on the Via Lucana (reverse direction).
- **Three weeks**: the Via Peuceta from Bari to Matera then the Via Ellenica to Brindisi, or the reverse. Otherwise, the Via Ellenica to Matera followed by the Via Lucana in reverse to Tricarico.
- **Four weeks**: the Via Ellenica from Brindisi to Matera, then the Via Peuceta in reverse to Bari. Catch the train back to Matera and proceed with the Via Lucana in reverse to Tricarico.

PLANNING YOUR WALK

The town of Matera

WHEN TO WALK

Spring (March–May) and autumn (September–October) are usually the best times and can be divine. The summer months are beautiful but frankly unsuitable as temperatures easily exceed 30°C and the dearth of shade makes it hot going. If you do opt for summer, to avoid sunstroke be prepared to set out at the crack of dawn when it's still cool, and rest during the middle hours of the day. Winter, on the other hand (November–February/March), means shorter days and often good walking conditions, although wet weather is a possibility.

WHERE TO STAY AND BOOKING

The majority of accommodation providers listed in this guidebook are associates of the CM and apply walkers' prices. However, as more new places open up, it's a good idea to check the listings on the official website (https://camminomaterano.it/strutture-ricettive). One of the beauties of the website is that you can see the location of accommodation. Please only use www.booking.com or other agencies if the CM listings are full.

Walkers enjoy a good range of comfortable lodgings, most with

Note: Italy goes onto daylight saving time from the end of March (when the clocks are set forward by one hour) to the end of October (clocks move back again by one hour).

Wi-Fi. Cosy B&Bs often turn out to be a renovated apartment in the historic heart of a village, a real privilege, while hostel-style accommodation may be provided in someone's house, and there is the occasional hotel in larger towns.

This guidebook uses the following symbols to represent different types of accommodation:

♠ hostel (shared dormitory and bathroom, maybe breakfast)

♻ hotel (breakfast is usually included)

♻ B&B (own room and bathroom, breakfast).

Obviously there are hybrid establishments too (see Appendix A for a list of accommodation along each route). **Note**: The price range is €25–35 per person, although a handful of places don't set a price for an overnight stay but instead specify 'donation'. Please be reasonable and respectful and leave at least €25 per person. Cash payment is usually preferred so check in advance if you wish to use a credit card.

If you'd rather not have to do the bookings yourself, the CM staff will do it on your behalf for the modest fee of €20. In this case, at least two weeks' advance booking is requested. Once you've registered (https://camminomaterano.it/booking-struttura), all you have to do is select your route and choose the category of accommodation you prefer for each stage. Payment is made directly to the accommodation provider.

If included, breakfast (*colazione*) is DIY (there'll be a tea/coffee maker and cakes/biscuits etc) or served by your host, or taken at a nearby café. Places with a kitchen mean you can do your own meals if preferred – there's always a local supermarket or grocery store (*alimentari*). Check with your host.

HOW MUCH MONEY SHOULD I BUDGET?

This will depend on the type of accommodation, but for a room with breakfast, picnic lunch and dinner with a drink, €50–60 per person should suffice, slightly less if you go for hostel options.

GETTING TO THE REGION

Both Bari (for the Via Peuceta) and Brindisi (for the Via Ellenica) can be reached from all over Europe by plane, train and long-distance bus, and Brindisi is also served by ferries from Greece. Seasonal flights from the USA land at both airports. Onward transport goes to Matera and beyond for the Via Lucana.

See the beginning of each chapter for more detail on getting to each route's starting location and then from the railway station or bus stop to the start of the walk.

RETURNING FROM MATERA

Either trains or buses can be used to leave Matera, and every town and village along the route has public transport. FAL trains (change at Altamura) go to Bari (https://ferrovieappulolucane.it/en) for onward connections with the rest of Italy on Trenitalia (www.trenitalia.com). By bus, you can travel direct from Matera to Bari airport thanks to Flixbus (www.flixbus.it).

HOW DO I SECURE MY CREDENTIAL AND TESTIMONIUM?

Akin to a walker's passport, the CM credential is compulsory. Apply on the CM website (https://camminomaterano.it/credenziale-del-pellegrino) or collect it at the start of each route. Your registration helps the organisation keep track of users and plan ahead.

> **Note**: The CM receives no public funding so please make a donation (€5 minimum per person) to cover costs and postage.

The credential is a bonus for walkers, enabling them to obtain discounts for accommodation and meals. It's also great fun collecting stamps (*timbri*); these are available in each village – see the corresponding route description for addresses, or ask your accommodation provider or the local rep.

The Cammino Materano credential

LOCAL REPS

The local volunteer reps (*referenti*) in each village deal with waymarking and path maintenance and are on hand to assist walkers; many are keen to show visitors around. Their contact details (for phone calls or WhatsApp messages) are listed at each relevant stage – but do remember they are volunteers and may not always be free.

The testimonium, on the other hand, certifies that you've walked the whole route. On presentation of your credential, duly filled with stamps, it can be collected at Matera (Statio Peregrinorum, Vico III Casalnuovo). Request it at least two days before your arrival through the local contact.

WHAT TO EAT AND DRINK

The best rule when eating out in a *ristorante*, *trattoria* or *osteria* is to ask what's on – *cosa avete oggi?* You'll undoubtedly be served flavoursome local specialities with seasonal products. Please don't request spag bol (you'd probably be ignored in any case) but be adventurous and appreciative.

In view of the extensive wheat cultivation in Puglia and Basilicata, it's understandable that bread (*pane*), pasta, pizza and focaccia are staples. Each village has its own original take and you'll enjoy a delicious range of unique products – crusty, soft, simple, topped with tomato, herbs, mozzarella, local sausage…perfect takeaway food for lunch. Bakeries often use olive cuttings to fire the ovens. Altamura and Laterza are especially famous for their bread. *Puccia* is a soft fat round roll typical of Bari.

Other snack food includes *pettole*, small fried balls of dough, both savoury and sweet, and *panzerotti*, folded pastry pockets stuffed with mozzarella and tomato and fried or baked. *Taralli* are crunchy swirls of oven-dried pastry often flavoured with *finocchio* (fennel seeds). Salamis and sausages are suitable picnic fare too. Flavoursome *capocollo* (using the pork neck) from Martina Franca is a special treat.

One veg not to be missed is *peperoni cruschi* (crunchy peppers), a Basilicata speciality. The slender sweet peppers are dried slowly over months then fried in extra virgin olive oil for a mini-fraction of a second before serving – they crumble and melt in your mouth. Another is *olive nolche*, soft black olives with a distinctively delicious bitter flavour.

Meat features prominently on menus, and butchers' shops (*macellerie*) often double as restaurants or takeaways for spit-roasted local meat, ranging from sausages to skewers of beef to *bombette*, cold pork cuts wrapped around a cheese mixture and grilled.

Clockwise from top left: focaccia comes in mouth-watering types; traditional Puglia orecchiette *pasta with greens and anchovies;* peperoni cruschi *peppers before drying; freshly made* mozzarella *cheeses; delicious* cartellate *made with fig syrup*

Although rare, seafood is not missing – the Adriatic Sea and the Gulf of Taranto are not far away. Pasta with *cozze* (mussels) with the addition of provolone cheese is a good one to try.

One stand-out pasta is *orecchiette* (round ear-like shapes, pressed with the thumb), traditionally served in Puglia with stewed *cime di rapa* (turnip greens) and flavoured with garlic and anchovies. In Basilicata, the topping of *mollica fritta* (fried breadcrumbs), *salsiccia* (sausage) and *peperoni cruschi* is common. In Cisternino, *orecchiette* made with roughly milled flour are called *recch' d'privt* (priest ears!).

Another pasta variety is *cavatelli* – elongated scooped-out shapes; then there are *troccoli*, freshly made and shaped like thin ribbons, *foglie di olive* (olive leaves), not to mention *strascinate*, *cicatelli*...the list is endless! A Bari speciality, *spaghetti all'assassina* (spaghetti made by a female killer!), are stewed in tomato sauce with garlic and a hit of fresh chilli until the liquid thickens and the pasta even burns a little!

Pancotto, also known as *puène quétte*, is a thick soup that uses up stale bread, which is cooked in broth; it comes with potatoes, onion, egg or tomato, depending on who makes it.

Vegetarian or not, you'll be sure to appreciate *fave con cicoria* – a smooth puree of fava beans served with slightly bitter greens. Other must-try veg include *friarielli*, tender leafy greens similar to *cime di rapa*; they go well with *salsiccia*. *Ceci* (chick peas) come in both black and yellow varieties, not to be confused with *cicerchie* (grass peas), cooked up as a soup with tomato and garlic. *Barattieri* taste like cucumbers but look like small melons and are often consumed as fruit. Other must-eat vegetables are artichokes – *carciofi*.

Mushrooms will hopefully include *cardoncelli*, lightly cooked and delicately flavoured. *Lampascioni* deserve a mention – these are tiny bitter wild onions considered a local delicacy, stewed in oil.

Cheeses are not in short supply, including soft fresh cow's milk mozzarella as well as *stracciatella* (no, not ice cream!), fat strings extracted from mozzarella and mixed with fresh cream. Rock caves are still used to store and age harder cheeses, as the cool and damp encourage the growth of mould, which adds flavour.

Figs are part and parcel of life here. In late summer, wayside trees with globule-like green and black figs encourage picking. Obviously they're delicious fresh as well as dried. Other wild fruit includes blackberries, pomegranates and fragrant almonds (but it goes without saying that you must follow the countryside rule of only gathering what's on common land and outside private property).

The dessert front is dominated by fragrant almond biscuits which come crunchy or chewy; an example are *vinarielli*. The locals also bake figs to

Freshly baked loaves at Laterza

produce an absolutely heavenly concentrated syrup, *cotto di fichi*, used on *cartellate*, sweet pastry rolls.

The Puglia and Basilicata regions produce memorable wines little known to visitors from overseas. Be prepared for pleasant surprises. Among the reds, you can expect to savour Primitivo di Manduria, Malvasia Nera, Negroamaro and Susumaniello (a ruby red wine from the Salento district), not forgetting Aglianico delle Vulture from Potenza. Whites include Fiano, Malvasia Bianca, refreshing Verdeca from Gravina and Locorotondo, and pale greenish-hued Greco. There are plenty of local rosés too – not sparkling and not sweet.

Beer is a mainstay. In Bari (and elsewhere), Peroni is synonymous with beer, and you'll often hear people ordering just that. After dinner, a tiny glass of *amaro* (digestive liqueur) is satisfying. The Amaro Lucano is a must, on a par with memorable Padre Peppe from Altamura, infused with walnuts, cinnamon and cloves.

Some trattorias and restaurants have a set price *menu pellegrino* (pilgrim menu) that costs around €15–20 – your accommodation provider can point you to these. Show your CM credential to be eligible. Always a good deal, it will include an array of locally sourced food, usually starting with mouth-watering *antipasti* (entrées), a meal in themselves.

The lane heading through fields towards Picciano in early summer
(VP Stage 6; photo: CM)

TOPOGRAPHY OF THE CAMMINO MATERANO

The Via Peuceta and Via Ellenica are best described as pretty flat near the coast then gently hilly followed by steepish, while the Via Lucana has stiffer and longer ups and downs.

One unavoidable negative note: the outskirts of several larger towns and the adjoining countryside are unfortunately despoiled by horrible amounts of rubbish dumped at random along the roadside. Local groups are working to resolve this problem.

GRAVINE

Puglia boasts over 60 canyons, or ravines, known as *gravine*, which are hundreds of metres deep and kilometres long. The sheltered conditions make them the perfect home for a wealth of plants, including endemic orchids, and wildlife galore. What's more, since time immemorial people have been living in this rugged environment, adapting natural caves as dwellings for themselves and stalls for their livestock, carving out churches and painstakingly frescoing them, and excavating rock for buildings above ground. Level land, albeit stony, was left for grazing and crop cultivation.

UNDERSTANDING LOCAL CULTURES

First and foremost, do find time to learn some Italian before you set out on your *cammino* and make the effort to greet people. *Buongiorno* (Good morning) is a good start, then there's *grazie* (thank you) and *arrivederci* (goodbye). People are extremely friendly and helpful, but outside tourist towns such as Bari, Brindisi, Alberobello or Matera they can't be expected to speak or understand English. The brilliant Google Translate app can always help you communicate.

All villages have a revered patron saint and celebrate their feast day. If you're lucky, you'll enjoy colourful processions when the saint's statue is carried around the village, crowds of people, local products, street food and great music, both traditional and modern. These are a real treat and entail an intriguing mix of pagan and sacred traditions sitting happily together.

Fascinating background reads are Carlo Levi's 1945 *Christ Stopped at Eboli* (also superbly filmed in 1979 by Francesco Rosi as *Cristo si è fermato a Eboli*, with Gian Maria Volonté – available with English subtitles) and Rocco Scotellaro's 1954 *Peasants of the South*. However, remember that both were written decades ago and a lot has changed. *Matera: The History of a Town* (Edizioni Giannatelli, 2016) by Lorenzo Rota is an in-depth study. Readers of Italian will appreciate *La Via dei Sassi* (Ediciclo, 2018), a walker's inspired account of the Via Peuceta, by Andrea Mattei.

PLANTS AND FLOWERS

Outstanding is the ferula or giant fennel (*Ferula communis*), a cumbersome umbrella-shaped plant, the tallest of its Mediterranean family. When dried, its thick stem has multitudinous uses, including scaffolding, furniture, bottle corks, walking sticks and shepherd's crooks. You might turn up your nose at the tiny snails that cluster on the plant stems, but people gather them and stew them with tomato.

Springtime walkers will be delighted by the vast carpets of wildflowers such as brilliant red poppies in the wheat fields, hedges of perfumed broom, pale yellow wild asparagus blooms, and tiny insect orchids. Aromatic Mediterranean herbs are year-round delights, releasing their scent when legs brush against them or boots tread on them: oregano, wild fennel, savory, mint, marjoram and thyme.

One hard-to-miss plant is squill (*Urginea maritima*), which grows widely across the countryside. Huge bulbs produce long leaves that quickly wither, to be replaced after summer by a tall spike clustered with pretty creamy-white blooms. Another unique plant is squirting cucumber (*Ecballium elaterium*). Encased in soft pointed leaves, modest yellow blooms keep company with hard cucumber-like seed pods that literally shoot off the plant and explode when ripe.

Walkers in late summer–autumn will be surprised by the colourful array of flowering plants such as yellow mustard and tiny purple autumn squill. Then there are lilac-pink meadow saffron, sky-blue chicory and straw-coloured teasel, not forgetting the pretty cyclamen flowers in the woods. A stand-out is golden yellow *Sternbergia lutea* or autumn crocus, with flowers like goblets. Delicately scented common smilax (*Smilax aspera*), with pretty white flowers, is dubbed *stracciabrache* or

'trouser ripper' for its insidious hidden thorns. Another curiosity is cocklebur (*Xanthium italicum*), a tall plant found on sandy wasteland, whose prickly burrs hook onto passersby – an inspiration for Velcro!

Don't ignore the trees and bushes along the way. Many are part and parcel of Mediterranean culture. Oaks come in a multitude of types, such as evergreen holm oak with its tiny glossy leaves and small acorns. The impressive carob tree has dangling dark edible seed pods, also known as St John's Bread. Almond trees are cultivated and fill fields with their

Clockwise from top left: squill can be recognised by its spikes with creamy flowers; woods are often carpeted with cyclamen; beautiful crocuses appear in autumn; curious squirting cucumber plant; an artistic dried teasel

delicate pink blossom in springtime, giving way to rock-hard nuts in late summer. The curious strawberry tree (*Arbutus unedo*) has shiny leaves and bears tiny ball-like fruit, often at the same time as its creamy bell blooms. Lentisc shrubs have dark green leaves and clusters of red berries.

Ancient gnarled olive tree (photo: LS)

Olives ripening

OLIVES

Olive trees are integral to Puglia. The region is Italy's most important producer of olives and boasts trees hundreds of years old, gnarled and sculpted by nature. Hailing from Asia Minor, the olive was 'discovered' by the Phoenicians and introduced to Italy by the Romans, although some claim evidence dating back to Mesolithic times (5000BC).

The olive features prominently in mythology: Athena is said to have planted a seed at the Acropolis which sprouted into a tree, providing the populace with a valuable source of wood for construction, as well as nutrition. For centuries, olive oil was used for lighting both homes and streets throughout the Mediterranean – right up to the time when electricity kicked in.

In Puglia, olive trees are found in extensive groves on the coastal plains and low inland hills, with snaking black plastic irrigation pipes ensuring a water supply. The trees are evergreen, and saplings take three to four years to produce fruit. Tiny pretty creamy blossoms appear amid the oblong grey–green leaves in spring, then the famous drupes ripen in late autumn–winter.

Several hundred olive varieties exist, but they all start off green then mature and darken into shiny purple–black as the months go by. If the harder green olives are preferred, they are picked as early as September. Freshly picked, they are extremely bitter and unappetising, and are best enjoyed after months soaking in water, brine and oil. Ripe black olives are slightly softer but more bitter and are preferred for oil.

The main harvest takes place in the winter months, usually October through to December. Workers use ladders to reach the highest branches, and nets are laid out beneath the trees so no fruit is lost. The harvest is taken to the nearest press where the olives are squashed whole, stones included, to extract the oil; this was traditionally done using massive round millstones turned by donkeys. The best version is cold-pressed *olio extravergine d'oliva*; deliciously fragrant when dribbled on salads, bread and much else, it is also excellent for cooking. Around 5–7 kilos of olives are needed to produce a single litre of oil.

Trees are pruned when the plant is resting, namely between harvest time and spring. The cuttings are often baled up and used to fire the region's bread ovens.

Visitors will be surprised to see withered and dying trees. The last 10 years have seen the slow but unfortunately inexorable spread of the insect-borne *Xylella fastidiosa* bacterium across Puglia. It ravages the olives, causing devastation in both economic and environmental terms; there is little growers can do except quarantine diseased exemplars and replace them.

WILDLIFE

Talk of birdlife on the CM must start with the ubiquitous chattering flocks of black jackdaws that nest in old masonry and town walls. Then there are the squawking European jays that act as woodland sentries, raising the alarm for other inhabitants. Skylarks often twitter and flutter over fields.

The sky itself is populated by surprising numbers of birds of prey, such as magnificent red and whistling kites and buzzards. Special mention is due to the lesser kestrel, known in Italian as the *falco grillaio* (cricket falcon), which devours the crickets and grasshoppers that are especially numerous in inland Puglia and Basilicata. Around a thousand breeding pairs have been recorded in Matera alone. One special but rare sighting is the elegant Egyptian vulture with its yellow face and white feathery hood and body with dark underwings. It migrates to southern Italy in spring–summer to nest in cliffs, usually in the ravines.

In terms of animals, the protected crested porcupine is especially shy and you'd be lucky to spot one, but chances are good of spotting the long black-and-white quills they drop. The ancient Romans, ever the epicures, introduced them to Italy from Africa as a banquet delicacy.

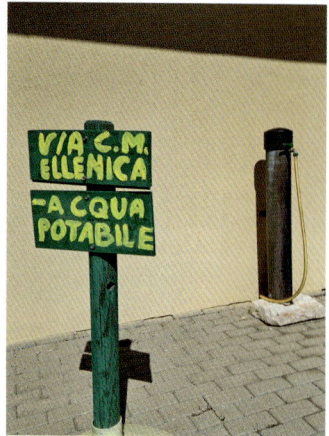

Drinking water for walkers (VE Stage 13)

WATER

Along with much of southern Italy, Puglia (or Apulia) has always been known as a dry region – the name means 'no rain' – so water has long been a strategic issue here. The late 1800s saw the first projects to deal with the shortage, and in 1906 construction began on a series of linked aqueducts to encourage farming and agriculture and to satisfy domestic and industrial demand. Fed by a network of springs, the mammoth Acquedotto Pugliese (AQP) has a main channel totalling 500km (the record holder in Europe), concluding with a monumental stepped cascade at the heel of Italy, Santa Maria di Leuca. The CM routes follow long stretches of the AQP.

One animal you have a chance of seeing is the wild boar (*cinghiale*). At 'worst' you'll see their hoofprints in the mud, although they can be confused with the slightly more slender roe deer prints. They're remarkably numerous in woodland, where they feast on acorns and roots, but they tend to be shy and dash off into the scrub to avoid contact with humans; it isn't a good idea to approach them if they have young. Foxes and even wolves are not unusual sightings either.

TRAINING FOR YOUR WALK

You'll want to enjoy your walk so will need to be fit enough to cover 15–30km each day on foot carrying a rucksack. The terrain varies from roads and flat land to undulating hills including some steep ups and downs, so plan your training period accordingly.

WHAT AND HOW TO PACK

Everyone has their own ideas about packing, but here are some considerations:

- Lightweight walking boots or trail shoes are more suitable than chunky mountain boots, which will make their weight felt on the sections of surfaced road. However, whatever you choose, make sure they protect and cushion your feet as there are lots of stony and rocky paths.
- Choose your rucksack carefully (25 litres is sufficient, believe me) and don't overload it. It needn't weigh more than 7kg.
- Two lightweight T-shirts, two pairs of undies and socks. Hint: when you wash your clothes at the end of the day's walking, wring them out then wrap them in a towel for 10min to speed up drying before hanging them out.

WALKING A CAMMINO

After a day or two, you fall into a relaxing rhythm…get up in the morning, breakfast, pack your toothbrush, shoulder your rucksack and head out the door. Follow lanes through fields and woodland, stopping to rest and refresh and drink in the scenery. There will inevitably be difficult days – your feet hurt, it's raining, your boots get muddy, you've taken a wrong turn – but it's all part of the experience. Accept everything that comes.

Then, at your destination, reward yourself with a refreshing drink at the café, locate your accommodation and meet your host, shower, wash your clothes, rest and sort through the day's photos – remembering to send a few to friends and family (not to make them envious of course). Embark on an exploratory wander around the village, pop out to dinner at a local eatery, roll into bed, start over again in the morning – and don't wipe that smile of satisfaction off your face.

- A lightweight fleece and an ultra-light down jacket if the season warrants it.
- A pair of shorts and a pair of long trousers.
- Waterproof gear – a poncho or rainproof jacket, overtrousers, rucksack cover and maybe a small umbrella if you wear glasses.
- Sun protection is very important. Shade is in short supply on the CM, so sunglasses and a large-brimmed hat, together with high-factor sun cream, are musts.
- Pack personal toiletries and essential medicines in small quantities.
- Trekking poles are not essential, but they do come in useful on rough rocky terrain and are also handy for discouraging over-enthusiastic dogs, not to mention scraping clay off your boots and for balance when crossing streams. However, remember that you can't transport them as cabin baggage on a plane.
- Two supermarket-sized plastic bags: muddy paths are a nuisance but wrapping plastic bags around your shoes can keep them cleaner and dry. Do take care not to slip!
- Drinking water is a crucial issue. A lightweight drinking bottle or bladder is essential, as fountains and taps are rare as hen's teeth in the countryside. It's good practice to drink plenty of water before you head out in the morning as well as carrying at least a litre with you. It goes without saying that you should fill up your bottle whenever water is available, mostly in villages.

BAGGAGE TRANSPORT

To have your luggage transported from stage to stage at the cost of €15 per bag (max 10kg) per person per stage, see https://camminomaterano.it/trasporto-zaini. The more people and bags, the lower the cost.

HEALTH AND WELL-BEING

The general emergency number in Italy is 112 (police), while 118 is for ambulance. Facilities at nearly all stage ends include a pharmacy (marked by a green cross above the door); by all means use these as reference points for medical issues, although they may recommend a local doctor or the hospital if necessary. The local reps can also be relied on for help.

For emergencies that require rescue when out on the trail, if the local contact can't help, use the handy app GeoResQ. If you have your tracking option on while walking and need help, once you've activated the call for help the app sends your position to the rescue team so you don't have to explain where you are.

The Via Ellenica reaches Bosco delle Pianelle (VE Stage 8)

ROUTE DESCRIPTIONS AND WAYMARKING

In the route descriptions, right and left are abbreviated as R and L, while compass directions are given as N, S, E, W (north, south, east, west). Cumulative distances are shown in **bold** at key intermediate points in each stage.

The information box preceding each stage gives:

- the location of the **start** and **finish**
- the approximate **time** required for the stage: this is 'skeleton' walking time, so always add on an hour or so to allow for rest stops, picnics, socialising...; if walking in a group, remember that the speed of the group is that of the slowest member
- **distance** (in kilometres)

- total **ascent** and **descent** (given in metres)
- **difficulty** – ranging from easy to moderate and moderately hard, depending on the distance, terrain, steepness and ascent/descent involved.
- **percentage paved** – approximately how much hard road surface you'll be walking on; for the most part these are quiet minor roads with little traffic.

The attractive colours of the CM signs were chosen as yellow (to symbolise wheat) and green (for the fields). These are found on clear painted stripes as well as arrows and stickers on lampposts, fences, rocks, trees, walls... Generally speaking, waymarking is pretty good on all routes, although as nature regains land, stretches do get

---

FREQUENTLY USED ITALIAN WORDS

A number of Italian terms are used throughout this guidebook. Those that occur most frequently are listed below, and an Italian–English glossary is provided in Appendix B.

cammino (plural: *cammini*)	long-distance walking route
duomo	cathedral
gravina (plural: *gravine*)	ravine, canyon shaped by flowing water
masseria (plural: *masserie*)	large old-style farm building
trullo (plural: *trulli*)	traditional cone-roofed hut in Puglia
via (plural: *vie*)	way, road, street

---

overgrown, and farmers and livestock inadvertently move stones.

The routes have been signed to enable walkers to follow them in either direction. Signs often say 'verso Matera' (towards Matera) or 'verso…' + other destinations. Make sure you follow the yellow arrows if heading for Matera (as per the route directions in this guidebook); otherwise, follow the green arrows if you choose the opposite direction, namely away from Matera.

MAPS, APPS AND GPX TRACKS

Currently there are no printed walking maps for the CM. This means that it's absolutely essential to set up an app (such as Gaia, Locus Map, AllTrails, Komoot, GeoResQ or Outdooractive) on your mobile phone, then download the GPX tracks for your chosen CM route. This way, you can check your position in relation to your walk whenever you're unsure about the

way to go. If your app has km markers, so much the better, although there are inevitably differences between individual apps, and between apps and the distances given in this book.

It's best to download GPX tracks from the official CM website, as these are kept updated; files are available from Cicerone too at www.cicerone. co.uk/1260/gpx. This may occasionally lead to minor differences from the maps in this guide as routes are modified locally.

A suggestion: while you're walking, don't have your phone out the whole time. Pop it in a pocket or your rucksack and only get it out when you need to check your position or take a photo. Otherwise, you'll find yourself looking at the screen constantly instead of marvelling at the scenery, and you'll find it harder to relax and get into your cammino rhythm. Holding your phone in your hand also increases the chances of tripping over.

VIA PEUCETA

The old heart of Bari with the cathedral (Stage 1; photo: JL)

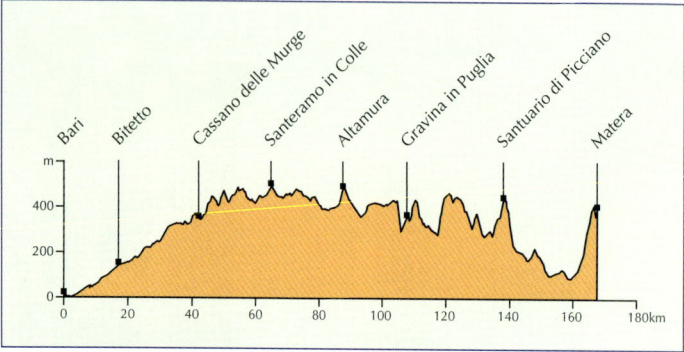

Start	Bari
Finish	Matera
Time	7 days (42hr)
Distance	167.5km
Ascent	2620m
Descent	2210m
Getting to Bari	Bari can easily be reached from cities all over Europe by train to Bari Centrale (www.trenitalia.com), long-distance Flixbus (www.flixbus.it) or plane (https://bari.airports.aeroportidipuglia.it); if arriving by plane, take the train or bus from the airport to the city.
Note	In the following route description, the Cammino Materano and Via Peuceta are abbreviated as CM and VP.

Getting to the Cammino start

From Bari Centrale railway station, take the main street Via Raffaele de Cesare due N past **Piazza Umberto I** and its park, continuing on **Via Andrea da Bari** to its conclusion. Turn R then first L (Via Benedetto Petrone) into Bari Vecchia, the historic part of town. Past the church of San Giuseppe, go second L then R and walk around the **Cattedrale di San Sabino**. Then Strada del Carmine leads on to where you enter Piazza San Nicola, with its statue of the great man and the **Basilica di San Nicola**, as well as the office for Cammino stamps. If in doubt about the way to go, ask – absolutely everyone knows where San Nicola is! Allow 30min for the 1.6km.

BARI 🔺 ⭕ 🍴 🏦 🏧 ➕ 🅷 ℹ️ ⏹️ ◉

LOCAL REP: MICHELE, TEL 347 7071064
STAMP: OFFICE ALONGSIDE BASILICA DI SAN NICOLA, PIAZZA SAN NICOLA
This sprawling dynamic historic city hums with life, especially in its innermost heart, a veritable maze of tiny alleys and streets. Boasting ancient origins, Bari thrived through Roman, Byzantine, Norman and medieval times, as testified by landmark monuments such as its Castello Normanno-Svevo and a string of churches. Don't miss the Basilica di San Nicola. The local saint – and precursor of Santa Claus – originally hailed from Myra in Turkey; his remains were whisked away by Bari seafarers in the 1100s, and are now revered in the crypt. Nicola replaced the city's former patron saint, San Sabino, who also has his own church.

Bari occupies a point sticking out into the harbour, facing the Adriatic Sea, with all that this entails – fishing, trade, navigation, migration. It lies a little over 200km across the water from the coast of Albania, and roughly the same distance from the heel of peninsular Italy. However, it also faces inland towards olive groves, wheat fields and vineyards. Just to be sure, the city erected all-encompassing fortifications to protect from incursions on all sides.

Bari

1 Habari We Dorm   2 B&B L'Ape che Gira   •••• route to Cammino start

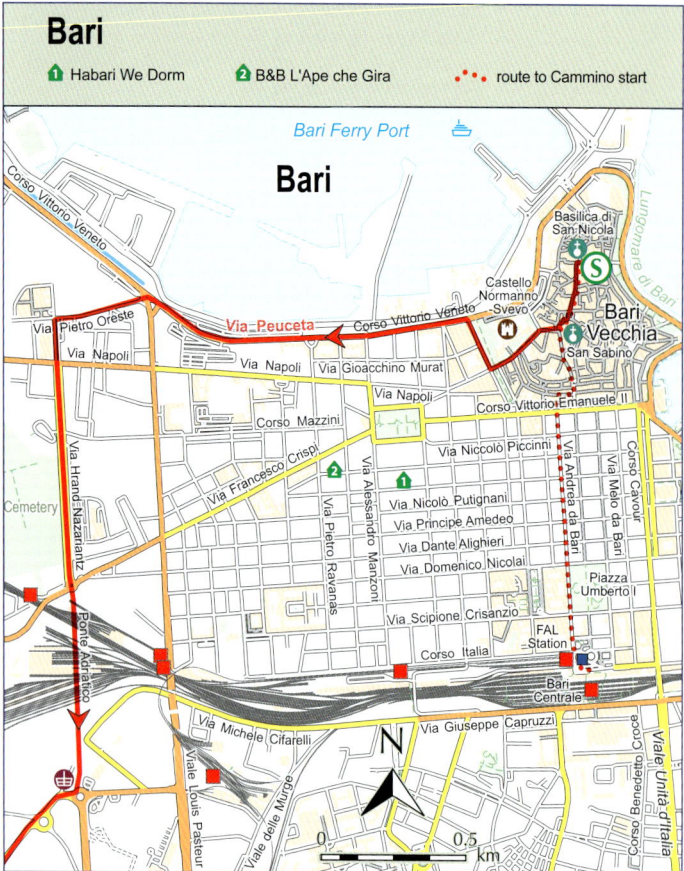

STAGE 1

Bari to Bitetto

Start	Basilica di San Nicola, Bari
Finish	Cattedrale di San Michele Arcangelo, Bitetto
Time	4hr 15min (1hr 45min via the variant from Modugno FS railway station)
Distance	17km (7km via the variant from Modugno FS railway station)
Total ascent	160m
Total descent	40m
Difficulty	Easy
Percentage paved	100%

The percentage of busy surfaced roads on this opening stage is quite frankly discouraging. After a short wander through the heart of the old town, you leave Bari on heavily trafficked roads, only reaching quieter rural areas after 8km. The recommended way to deal with this is to visit Bari first, explore the warren of narrow streets and monuments, get your Cammino stamp, then catch a Ferrovie dello Stato (FS) train to Modugno: see variant from Modugno described in Stage 1. From there, you slot into the main route via tranquil country roads, touching on archaeological sites and passing through extensive olive groves the rest of the way to Bitetto.

BITETTO – GET THE NAME RIGHT!

Make sure you end up in the right place today, as confusingly the outskirts of Bari also include very similarly named Bitonto, Binetto and Bitritto, as well as Bitetto (that's the one you want)!

From the Basilica di San Nicola in Bari (5m), face his statue and take the street to its L then immediately go L again on Strada del Carmine. Stick with this, passing churches, cafés and shops as far as the huge Romanesque **Cattedrale di San Sabino**. Here, bear R through its square and on to reach the magnificent **Castello Normanno-Svevo** and museum. Keep L along its walls then R past gardens out to traffic lights on the portside. Turn L now on a cycle track flanking busy **Corso**

Vittorio Veneto past docks for 2km to where arrow stickers on poles tell you to cross over for **Via Pietro Oreste**. Some 300m on, branch L on a wide avenue past a Telecom building to a **cemetery**, then cross over rail tracks on the magnificent modern **Ponte Adriatico**.

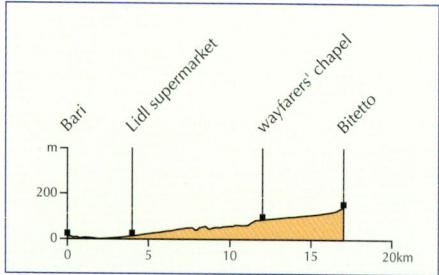

Once on the other side, at the Lidl super-market (**4km**), go R then L (Strada Santa Caterina) then straight ahead passing industrial areas on a rub-bish-strewn road, heading over a railway line and past fields. Cross a roundabout and continue through a commercial area, keeping to an awkward path on the right of the road. At the next roundabout, in the midst of a shopping centre (the last opportunity for refresh-ments), take the busy road signed for Brindisi over a **viaduct** (**6.5km**). Take great care on this busy stretch with virtually no sidewalk! Go straight ahead (sign for

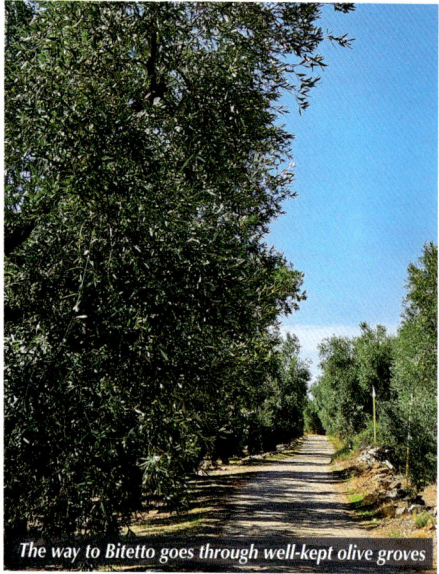

The way to Bitetto goes through well-kept olive groves

Modugno). At the next intersection, keep R below a larger road before curving uphill, where you turn sharp R on the **Strada Antica Modugno** (**8km**).

Things quieten down considerably now so you can find your cammino pace and enjoy the walking from here on. Olive groves and orchards lined with prickly pears occupy the stony terrain. Pass under a viaduct (**A14**) then head past the **Janfko rest area** (**9.2km**). At a road junction, the way bears S past a vineyard fol-lowing a *lama*, a broad shallow canyon shaped by long-gone flowing water. At a

map continues on p48

T-junction (**11km**), go R then L and slightly uphill past an AC Milan football acad-emy, then branch R to a bench and tiny 1759 **wayfarers' chapel** (**12km**), where the variant from Modugno slots in.

Variant from Modugno FS railway station

Note: Make sure you catch the FS train to Modugno – the station is located on the southern side of town. (Another railway, operated by Ferrovie Apule Lucane, FAL, delivers you to the opposite side of Modugno, a little further away from the VP; however, waymarking points you through.)

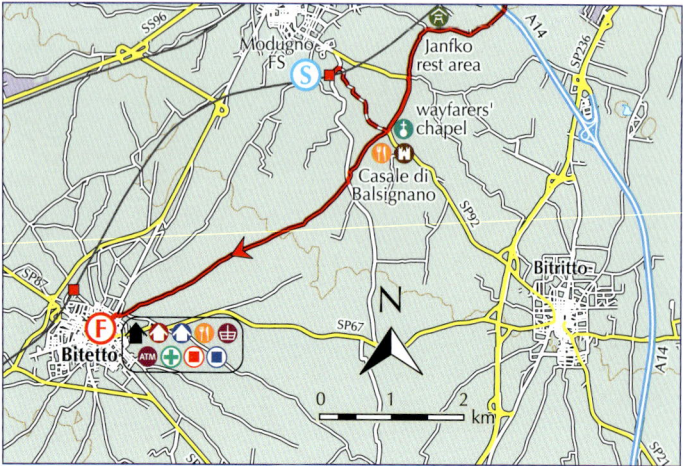

From Modugno FS station car park, turn R following CM stickers. Keep L, parallel to the railway line, until you're pointed R on a lane through an olive plantation and over the railway (which runs in a tunnel here so you don't notice it). A quiet minor road SSE passes a series of colourfully decorated rest areas, courtesy of local volunteers (the Sentieri Modugnesi, SM). A conical *trullo* hut in a field (see 'Trulli' box in Stage 2) marks a Neolithic settlement dating back to 6000–4000BC. Not far on is the 1759 **wayfarers' chapel** (**2km**), where you join the main VP.

Main route continues

A worthwhile 5min detour L leads to **Casale di Balsignano** (www.casaled-ibalsignano.it), a fortified medieval settlement with a tower, frescoed chapel and visitor centre with Cammino stamps, WC, refreshments and picnic area. After visiting, retrace your steps to the main route.

Branch R flanking the low stone wall of **Casale di Balsignano** and go straight on at a partially completed road junction, pass a barrier and under power lines, then head on SW through olives, olives, olives and shady fig trees. After parting ways with the SM route, cross over a road and pass under more power lines. All of a sudden you're on the edge of Bitetto, and the inspiring majolica-tiled dome of the church appears.

Take the third turn L into town. You're led through an arch into the delightful old quarter and Piazzetta Portapiscina. Follow narrow paved Via XXIV Maggio through to the main square and breathtaking Romanesque cathedral San Michele Arcangelo, its entrance door guarded by stone lions. Opposite is an elegant palazzo with a clock tower. You're in **Bitetto** (140m, **17km**).

BITETTO 🏠 🔵 🔵 🍴 🚆 🏧 ➕ 🔴 🔵
LOCAL REP: ESTER, TEL 340 6051347
STAMP: THE CATHEDRAL; CAFFÈ ROMA, PIAZZA ROMA 5
Once you've settled into your accommodation, go for a wander along the atmospheric narrow paved streets with their arched passageways.

Carved arch at Casale di Balsignano

STAGE 2
Bitetto to Cassano delle Murge

Start	Cattedrale di San Michele Arcangelo, Bitetto
Finish	Piazza Aldo Moro, Cassano delle Murge
Time	6hr 15min
Distance	25km
Total ascent	300m
Total descent	100m
Difficulty	Moderate
Percentage paved	55%

A rather long but enjoyable stage that rambles out into the countryside. In the company of a sea of olive trees, almond orchards and grapevines, it crosses innumerable lanes and makes over 25 right-angle turns! The way climbs very gently towards the Altopiano delle Murge, which will be the dominant landscape for the days ahead. Signage and landmarks are not always abundant today, so keep your GPX files on hand.

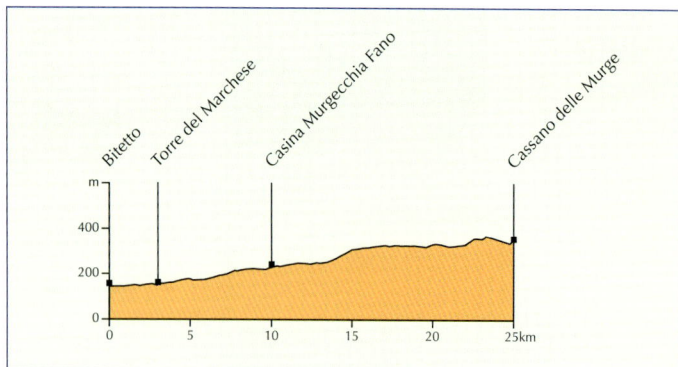

Facing the cathedral in Bitetto, go R (SSW) to the roundabout then take Via Garibaldi past the church of **Santa Maria della Veterana**, heading S all the way out

The Via Peuceta passes the Torre del Marchese

of town. Cross straight over a **main road** (**0.9km**) then branch L through a peaceful landscape of fields and olive plantations edged with low stone walls. At a T-junction keep L on an unsurfaced lane around a building and take a path up past the remains of an old tower-like farm building, the **Torre del Marchese** (**3km**). Turn sharp R here.

Curve S then veer SW at first on a surfaced road which crosses the Acquedotto Pugliese multiple times. See 'Water' box in the Introduction. Continue on to cross over **railway lines** (**8km**), then 500m further on turn L at a T-junction. Pass the large house **Casina Murgecchia Fano** (**10km**), then a trullo, then **turn abruptly R** (**13km**) as you approach a disused building. To the south is a substantial area of greenhouses.

map continues on p52

51

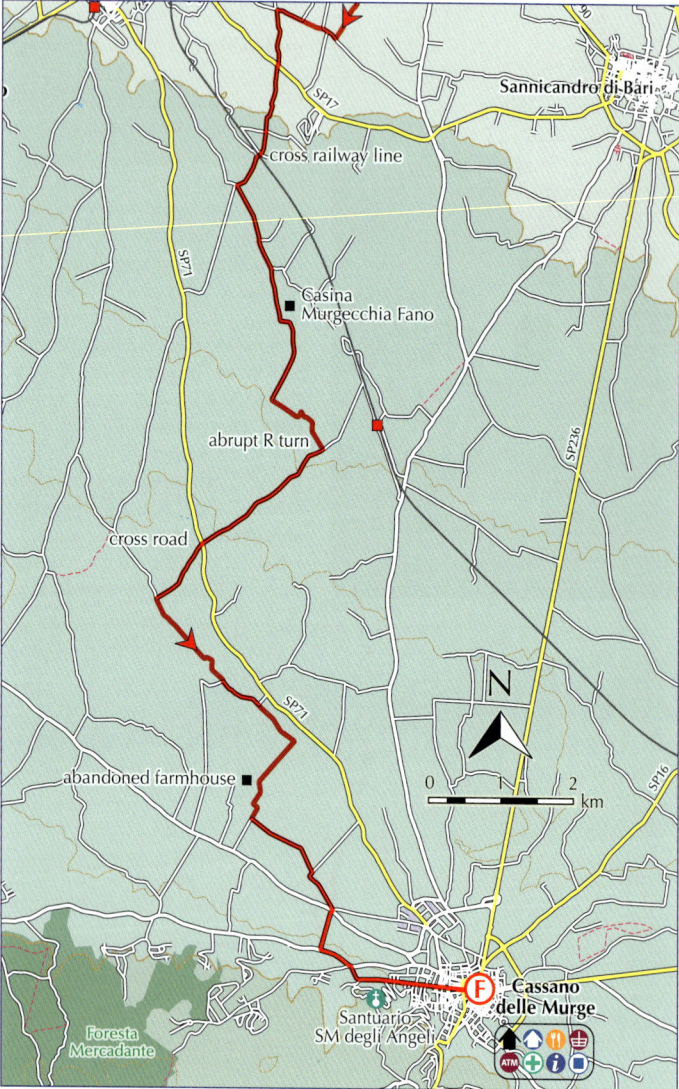

Sannicandro di Bari

cross railway line

Casina
Murgecchia Fano

abrupt R turn

cross road

abandoned farmhouse

Cassano
delle Murge

Santuario
SM degli Angeli

Foresta
Mercadante

N

0   1   2 km

TRULLI

So typical of southern Puglia, *trulli* (singular *trullo*) are unique conical stone huts like doll's houses. Originally used as shelter or sheds for farmers, they probably derive their name from the Greek for 'dome'. No two are the same. Tiled roofs perch atop curious small huts constructed with the drystone technique using local limestone rock. The topmost point is often decorated with pagan symbols and inscriptions in white ash, intended to keep evil spirits away.

Many stood in ruins but are gradually being restored and converted into homes and tourist accommodation; it's a real treat to stay in one. Several trulli modules are often joined by masonry, and there are even trullo churches.

Continue SW through farmland and **cross a road** (**15km**) then swing SE. After an **abandoned farmhouse** (**20km**), the VP starts to gently descend past oak trees, with distant views of the Murge plateau for the first time. Cross a road junction (**22km**) and climb on a dispiriting wide road. Go L (signed for Cassano) and over a roundabout (**23km**) then R. This road leads past the hillside home to **Santuario Santa Maria degli Angeli** and all the way into the centre of town, through Piazza Garibaldi and up alongside the fine church (Santa Maria Assunta) to Piazza Aldo Moro in **Cassano delle Murge** (340m, **25km**).

CASSANO DELLE MURGE ⬆ ⭕ 🍴 ⛪ ATM ➕ ℹ️ 🏛️
LOCAL REP: PAOLO, TEL 388 6074723
STAMP: BAR PRINCIPE, PIAZZA ALDO MORO; TOURIST INFO, VIA MIANI 11
On the easternmost edge of the Parco Nazionale dell'Alta Murgia, Cassano delle Murge is a bustling place with a lively square; the church is the architectural centrepiece. The town has prehistoric origins and flourished in Roman times. It may be named after Cassius, a leader in the plot to assassinate Julius Caesar. Cassano is also renowned among walkers for the Pecora Nera pub, home of the CM's 'fake' patron saint, Sant'Eulgio (see Introduction).

STAGE 3
Cassano delle Murge to Santeramo in Colle

Start	Piazza Aldo Moro, Cassano delle Murge
Finish	Piazza Garibaldi, Santeramo in Colle
Time	5hr 45min
Distance	22.5km
Total ascent	420m
Total descent	240m
Difficulty	Moderate
Percentage paved	55%

The VP really hits its stride on this stage. It climbs onto the rugged limestone Murge plateau with lots of flourishing oak woods, home to boar, which adore the plentiful acorns. There are also plenty of open fields edged with drystone walls, and later mixed farms. The Murge covers some 4000km^2 in all and is pitted with cave dwellings, stables, old churches and monasteries. Refreshments are available at several places en route.

From Piazza Aldo Moro in Cassano delle Murge, facing away from the church, go R on narrow Via Carlo Chimienti past houses and across a road, and after

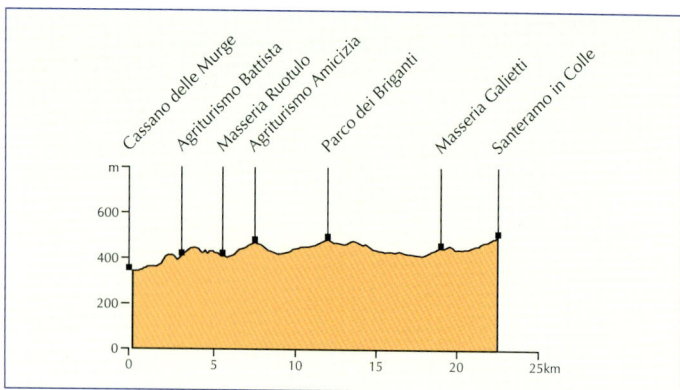

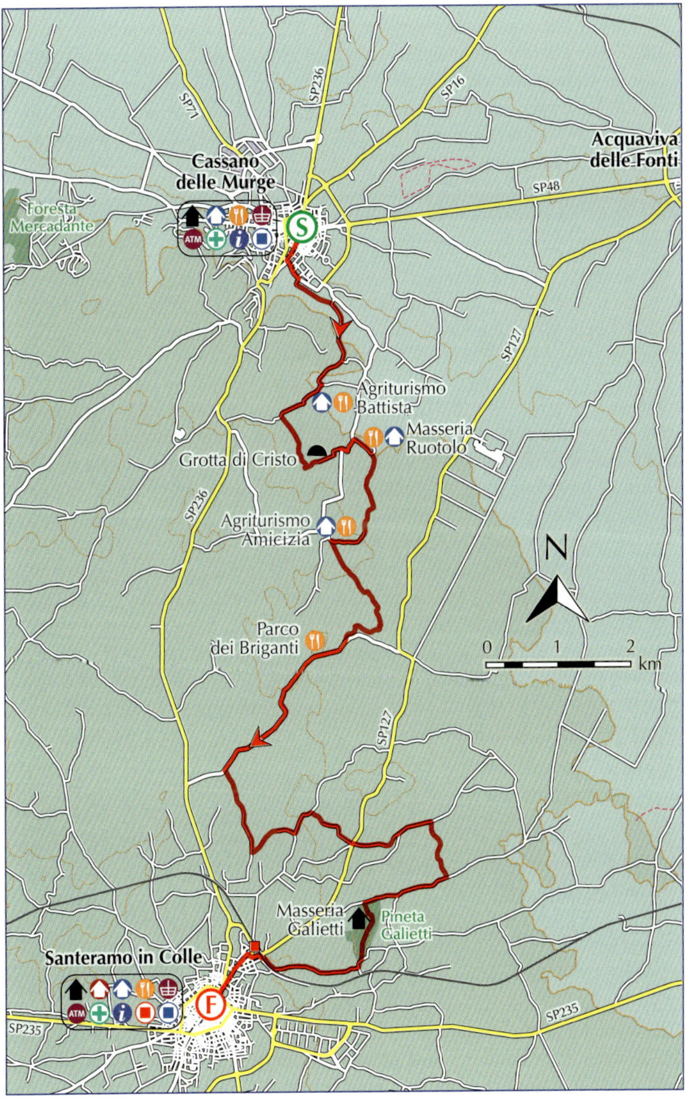
SP71
SP236
SP16
Acquaviva delle Fonti
Cassano delle Murge
SP48
Foresta Mercadante
ATM
SP127
Agriturismo Battista
Masseria Ruotolo
Grotta di Cristo
SP236
Agriturismo Amicizia
N
Parco dei Briganti
0
1
2
km
SP127
Masseria Galietti
Pineta Galietti
Santeramo in Colle
ATM
SP235
SP235

500m turn L and pass a spa complex. After 100m turn R up a rough road which bends L past a barrier, then continue along an embankment above the Acquedotto Pugliese. Follow this for a further 750m and turn R onto a road which climbs surprisingly steeply. An intricate series of roads and tracks now proceed broadly S with many well-signed right-angle turns – it's well worth keeping an alert lookout for signage, combined with the GPX track.

DRYSTONE WALLS

Farmers have spent centuries labouring to clear the rocky land to make it suitable for grazing and agriculture. Over time, the stones removed were heaped up carefully along the edges of fields, zigzagging across the landscape, little-recognised masterpieces of construction without cement.

Pass ⟳ **Agriturismo Battista** (**3km**, refreshments) and 500m further go L onto a track alongside the walled property. The way soon narrows and may be overgrown, descending and climbing again. Pass a sign to the **Grotta di Cristo** (**4.7km**), a limestone cave in a dolina believed to have been inhabited in prehistoric times. After a sharp turn L you emerge on a road and turn R through luxury resort ⟳ **Masseria Ruotolo** (**5.5km**, refreshments).

Continue downhill on good paths S through the woods of the Bosco della Mesola to ⟳ **Agriturismo Amicizia** (**7.5km**, refreshments). Turn sharp L on a gravel lane which crosses fields and joins a walled pathway through more trees, with livestock gates. Look out for a R turn through an awkward gap in the wall (**9km**). Follow through woods to join a road, branching R. Pass the **Parco dei Briganti** play area (refreshments) and continue to a fork L (**13km**) onto a wide dusty lane to a quarry. Follow a path between stone walls then go L on a road (**14.3km**).

SHORTCUT

By turning R you will be in **Santeramo in Colle** inside an hour. However, the official route makes an attractive loop through farms and forests, taking a further 2hr.

After 500m go R onto a narrow shaded path between walls. Cross a busy road and follow roads and tracks to a fork R (**16.7km**). Turn R to join a road for just over 1km to a L turn onto the avenue through **Pineta Galietti** (**19km**) pine wood, passing the impressive buildings of ⌂ **Masseria Galietti**. Leave the wood past a green gate and turn R along the road that leads to the outskirts of Santeramo.

Follow waymarks over the railway line to a roundabout with a bar and turn L on Via Stazione, up past the elegant gardens of Piazza Vagno. Then narrow Via F Netti leads into the old town centre and the stage end at Piazza Garibaldi in **Santeramo in Colle** (500m, **22.5km**).

SANTERAMO IN COLLE 🏠 ⬡ ⬡ 🍴 ⊕ ATM ✚ ℹ ⬛ ⬛

LOCAL REP: GIUSEPPE, TEL 338 9980586

STAMP: BAR ITALIA, PIAZZA GIUSEPPE DI VAGNO; TOURIST OFFICE, PIAZZA GARIBALDI

Santeramo (accent the second syllable) is a fairly typical country town with a maze of narrow paved streets which unexpectedly emerge into a spacious square, Piazza Garibaldi, with its church, cafés and shady benches where local people gather to pass the time of day. Not a high-rise to be seen but instead rows of neat pale-cream two- to three-storey houses, each with an artistic wrought-iron balcony and front doors opening onto the street, often via a flight of stone steps.

Not an easy place to be a vegetarian, Santeramo is renowned for its meat, featured in restaurants and *macellerie* (butcher's shops) equipped with non-stop spit roasts and BBQed meat on grills.

Arrival in Santeramo in Colle

STAGE 4
Santeramo in Colle to Altamura

Start	Piazza Garibaldi, Santeramo in Colle
Finish	Piazza Duomo, Altamura
Time	5hr 45min
Distance	23km
Total ascent	290m
Total descent	300m
Difficulty	Moderate
Percentage paved	40%

An especially enjoyable stage with plenty of varied landscapes, starting with fields of wheat then arid steppe-like land with vast horizons and solid stone *masseria* farms. Aromatic herbs are plentiful. An ancient road over rock carved with grooves is another delight. Navigating is easier on this section as the VP straightens out on its way west to Altamura. Refreshments are possible at Masseria Scalera.

Head uphill from Piazza Garibaldi in Santeramo in Colle on Via Roma, and turn R at the park along the side of the grand building of the Municipio. After 200m turn L then R and follow Via Redipuglia as it gradually descends. After a school, take the next L. You are now outside the town.

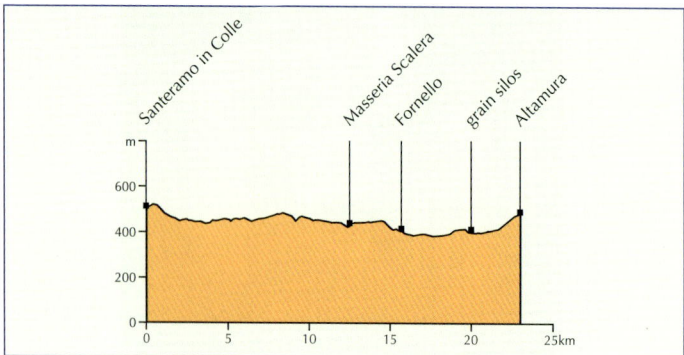

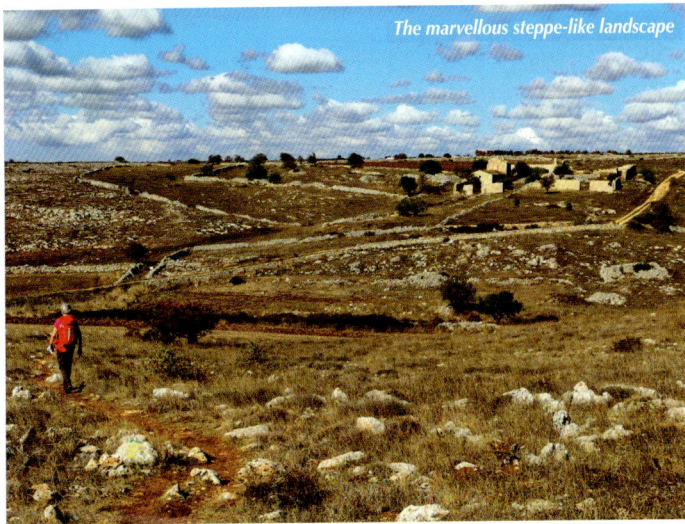

The marvellous steppe-like landscape

The road becomes a lane between stone walls before the VP turns L on a road (**3km**) and heads under **railway tracks**, keeping L. At **4.8km** go straight on, leaving the tarmac for a series of lanes then stretches of road. The VP enters an open area of wild steppe and heads downhill towards a distant mast, past trulli and across exposed and lightly farmed land. Turn L in descent (**9km**) before climbing on uneven rocky terrain to join a lane passing an isolated farm. This section of the Murgia plateau is high and flat, with extensive views everywhere you look.

Heading steadily W, descend on a road to dairy farm **Masseria Scalera** (**12.5km**, refreshments) then ascend past upmarket Villa Ninfea and Masseria La Meridiana (**15.7km**). Continue over the level plateau, with Altamura coming into view as you start to descend. The VP follows old cart grooves in the limestone pavement to a crater housing the erstwhile cave settlement of **Fornello** (**15.7km**). You then proceed across a rich arable plain. Keep R at the **railway** and follow it before crossing. Crest a small ridge and pass a group of big **grain silos** (**20km**).

At a road, turn R twice, skirting the town, before passing under a main road (**21km**). Keep walking in the same direction to meet a larger road, Via Cassano delle Murge, and follow this L (SW) as it heads up into town. Cross a larger road and proceed on Via Genova past the archaeological museum. At a small square bear R along a small alley to finally emerge in modest Piazza Duomo, **Altamura** (475m, **23km**).

ALTAMURA ⬡ ⬡ 🍴 ⛪ 🏧 ✚ 🛈 🔲 🔳

LOCAL REP: GIOVANNI, TEL 328 9254928
STAMP: PRO LOCO, PIAZZA REPUBBLICA 11

Altamura is an ancient town sporting pre-Roman walls, abandoned following Saracen raids and later reconstructed royally by Frederick II, Duke of Swabia, King of Sicily and Holy Roman Emperor, to quote but three of his titles! He is celebrated in late April every year at 'Federicus', an event-packed three-day medieval festival, when the whole town dons costumes.

As well as feasting on bread and focaccia, visitors should wander along the warren of alleyways and tiny squares called *claustra*. Don't miss the superb Romanesque churches, in particular the 13th-century cathedral. Try to fit in a visit to Palazzo Baldassare for the exhibition about the fossilised skeleton of Neanderthal 'Uomo di Altamura' – the man himself is literally imprisoned in the limestone of the nearby Lamalunga cave (www.uomodialtamura.it). The museum also has information regarding 30–40,000 dinosaur footprints (80 million years old) discovered in a nearby quarry.

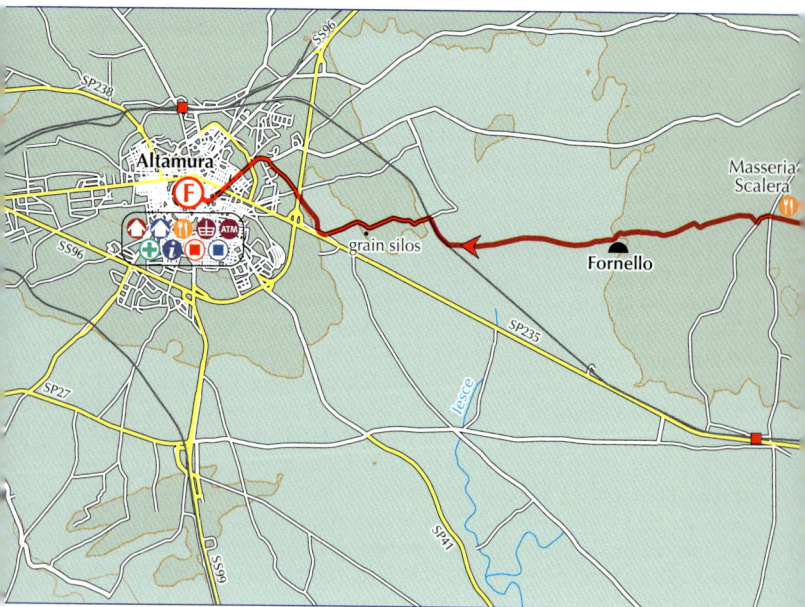

BREAD, FOCACCIA AND...HAMBURGERS

In 37BC the Roman poet Orazio (Horace) praised the *pane di Altamura* (bread of Altamura) as the best he'd ever tasted. The town has made a trademark of its special bread. Some of the current bakeries have existed here for over 600 years – Antico Forno Santa Chiara opened in 1423 and is still going strong. Crusty 1kg loaves made from local hard durum wheat semolina are baked in massive ovens fired with oak wood; the bread lasts up to two weeks.

A popular version of lightly leavened bread found in different versions all over Puglia is focaccia, a sort of soft pizza baked with oil and light toppings. And that brings us to a curious (true) story. In 2001 the fast-food chain McDonald's opened its first outlet in the centre of Altamura, and soon afterwards two local baker brothers opened a *focacceria* nearby. The latter attracted floods of customers, and in less than a year since opening, the hamburger joint closed shop, a victory for traditional cuisine. The story made it onto the pages of international newspapers, and foreign journalists flocked to Altamura. The hilarious film *Focaccia Blues* came out in 2009.

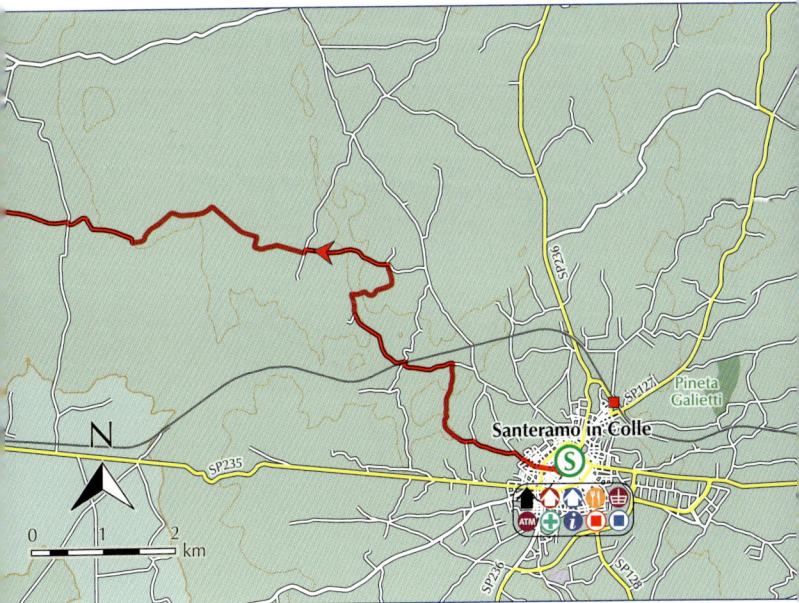

STAGE 5
Altamura to Gravina in Puglia

Start	Piazza Duomo, Altamura
Finish	Belvedere near the cathedral, Gravina in Puglia
Time	5hr
Distance	20km
Total ascent	200m
Total descent	340m
Difficulty	Easy–moderate
Percentage paved	40%

Not especially tiring, this stage crosses open fields with solar farms and distant views of towering grain silos – the wheat has to go somewhere. You will get to Gravina in Puglia in plenty of time to visit this fascinating and historic town.

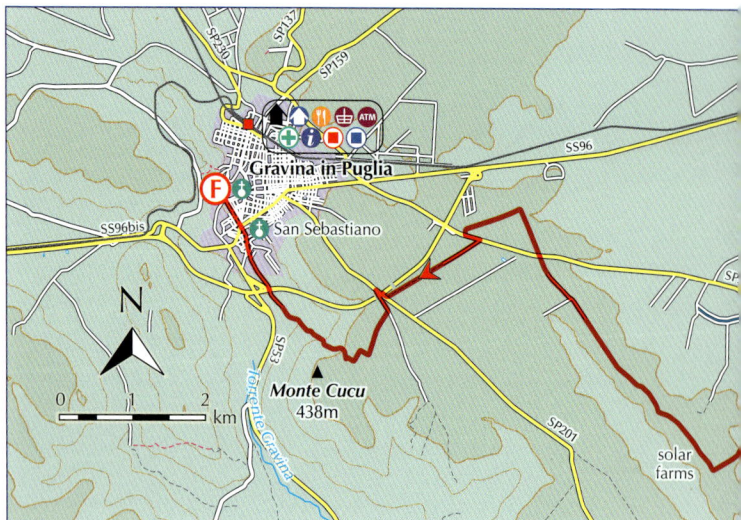

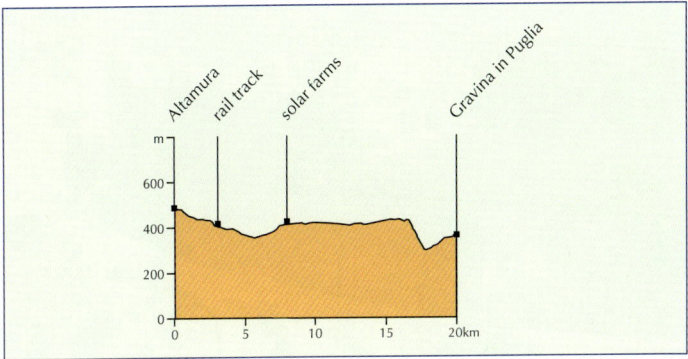

From Piazza Duomo in Altamura, head S on Corso Federico II di Svevia. Where it ends, go R on Via Garibaldi. Pass around a small park and continue on Via Selva, keeping R at a split in the road (**1km**). Pass through suburban developments and under the **SS96 road** in a tunnel. Branch R into open country, passing sizeable quarries. Turn L under the **rail track** (**3km**) then soon L off the road.

A lane now leads S through wheat fields and across a busy road. Keep ahead

over a **water channel** (**5.6km**) and continue on the farm track. After a sharp R (**8km**), the VP proceeds past **solar farms** and across the busy road again (**11.7km**). Follow waymarks and GPX, looping back to join the road briefly before heading back out into the countryside. When you meet the road again (**15km**), you double back for a series of twists and turns, rising below **Monte Cucu**, until quite suddenly spectacular views open up across to Gravina.

Descend on the path NW through woods before more uphill, pass under a road then take a direct line past the **church of San Sebastiano** into the narrow streets of the town centre. Head under

63

Gravina and its wonderful Ponte Acquedotto

an archway at Piazza Pellicciari and onwards to a L turn for spacious Piazza Benedetto XIII with the cathedral. At the end is the marvellous Belvedere view-point of **Gravina in Puglia** (340m, **20km**), with the steep-sided gorge pitted with cave dwellings spread out before you, spanned by the Ponte Acquedotto.

GRAVINA IN PUGLIA 🔼 🔵 🟠 🔵 🔵 ➕ 🔵 🔴 🔵

LOCAL REPS: LEO, TEL 339 7943945; ROSA, TEL 380 7676235
STAMP: THE CATHEDRAL OR THE LOCAL REPS

Aptly, the name Gravina means 'canyon'; after vandals destroyed the town in AD456, it became home to the local populace, who developed extensive cave settlements including multi-layered houses, stalls for livestock, storage areas and chapels.

The striking 37m-high Ponte Acquedotto spans the awesome canyon, leading to the archaeological area. The bridge can be admired in the spectacular opening sequences of the 2021 James Bond film *No Time to Die*. It dates back to the 13th century under Frederick II, when a castle was also built for hunting parties in the Murgia. He reportedly called Gravina 'a garden of delights', and it is still known to many Italians as '*la città di Federico*' for his contribution to the stately buildings, many of them now home to colonies of chattering jackdaws that circle in vast noisy clouds. The town also flourished at length under the Orsini lords in the 15th–19th centuries. Find time for the Gravina *sotterranea* (underground) visit, to see where the tufa rock was excavated to construct the town.

STAGE 6
Gravina in Puglia to Santuario di Picciano

Start	Belvedere, Gravina in Puglia
Finish	Santuario di Picciano
Time	7hr 30min
Distance	30.3km
Total ascent	720m
Total descent	620m
Difficulty	Moderately hard
Percentage paved	35%

Very enjoyable, if long, this stage spends its time in woods and rolling farmland where wheat is cultivated. Be aware that in wet weather, sections of the stage (the second half in particular) get awfully muddy. Do consider alternatives, otherwise allow plenty of extra time.

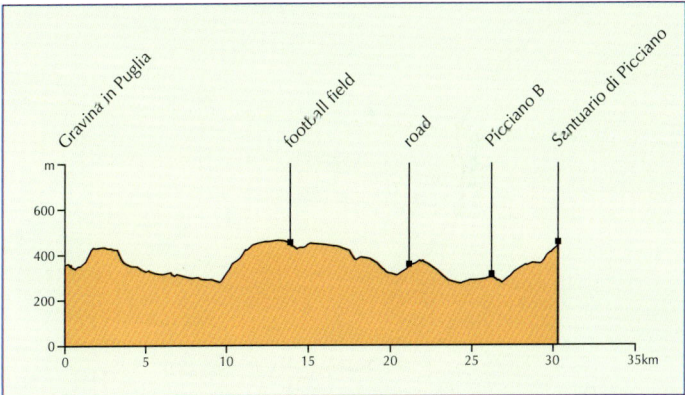

Note: Stages 6 and 7 can be shortened by asking the Gravina reps to drive you part of the way.

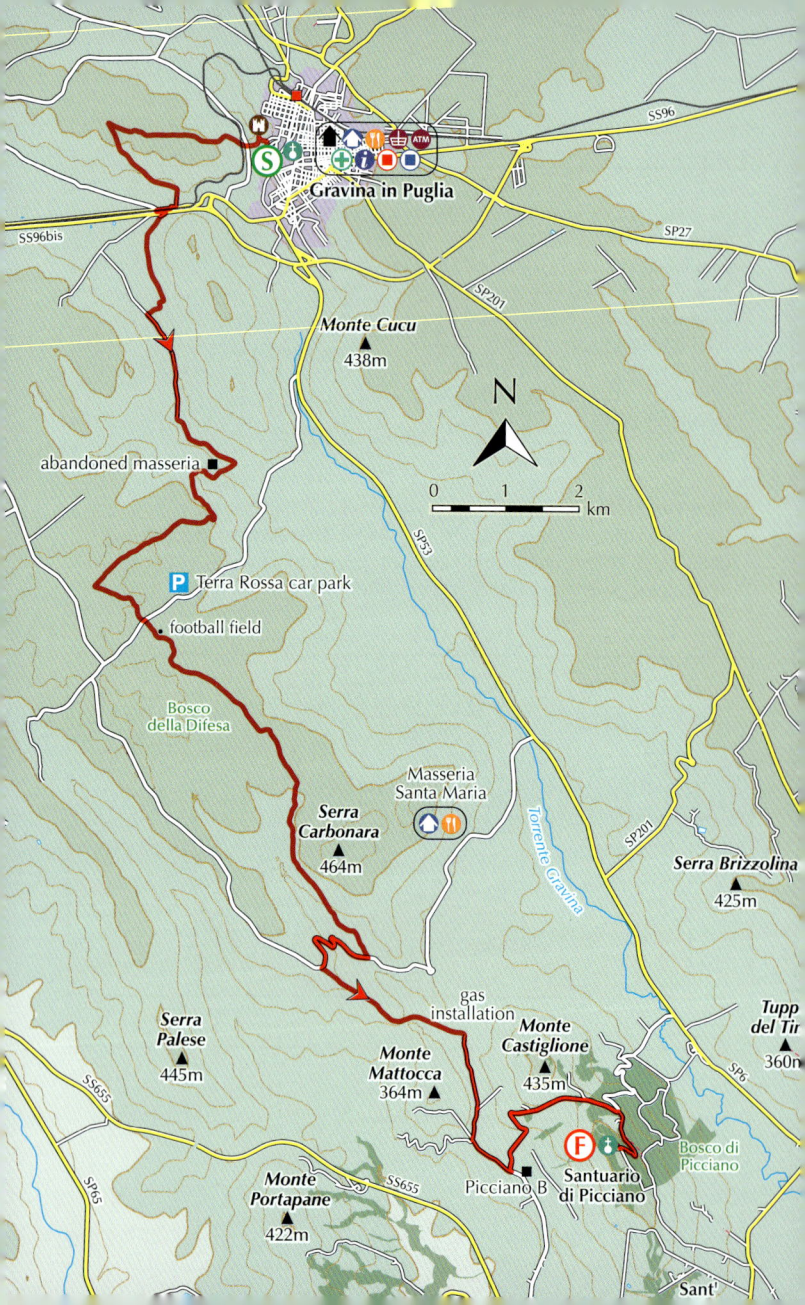

Gravina in Puglia

Monte Cucu
438m

N

0   1   2 km

abandoned masseria ■

P Terra Rossa car park

• football field

Bosco della Difesa

Serra Carbonara ▲
464m

Masseria Santa Maria

Torrente Gravina

Serra Brizzolina ▲
425m

Serra Palese ▲
445m

gas installation

Monte Castiglione ▲
435m

Tupp del Tir ▲
360n

Monte Mattocca ▲
364m ▲

Monte Portapane ▲
422m

Picciano B ■

F Santuario di Picciano

Bosco di Picciano

Sant'

SS96

SS96bis

SP27

SP201

SP53

SP201

SP6

SS655

SP65

SS655

From the Belvedere in Gravina in Puglia, walk through the piazza; after the church on the corner, go L then L again on Via San Basilio. This curves back towards the gravina and reaches another viewpoint where the road ends. Now steps lead down to the marvellous **Ponte Acquedotto** (**0.5km**).

Cross over and climb up, looping past an old rock church with an awesome outlook back to Gravina. Take a lane bearing W across a road then a **railway line** (**1.3km**); the lane levels out as it crosses wheat fields. A fine trullo stands out on your R above a substantial valley, then a signed fork points you sharp L down over the **SS96bis road** (**5km**). Continue S cross-country, then branch L on a tarmacked road (**6.8km**) following a stream lined with rushes and trees. A leisurely lane takes over before the VP veers R to climb past a large **abandoned masseria farm** (**10km**) on the edge of the historic Bosco della Difesa, an extensive forest of pines, cypresses, oaks and much else.

> Incredibly, between 1960 and 1962 during the Cold War years, an intercontinental missile base was constructed in the **Bosco della Difesa**, one of 10 in the Puglia and Basilicata regions. It was reportedly struck by lightning on several occasions…miraculously without dire consequences!

Clearly marked paths and tracks continue uphill, mostly S, to emerge onto a plateau, before veering briefly SE to cross a road (**13.8km**) near the **Terra Rossa car park** (handy for walkers splitting the stage). Proceed through the forest, more open here, past an unexpected **football field** (**15km**) and SE for the most part, keeping an eye out at the many path and lane junctions. There's a gentle downhill through

You walk up towards Bosco della Difesa

The lane heading through fields towards Picciano in autumn

eucalypts, then more ups and downs at the foot of Serra Carbonara until the VP finally leaves the wood as it meets a **road** (**20.2km**). (Turn L here for ⭘ Masseria Santa Maria, refreshments). Go R and follow the sweeping curves uphill to pick up a lane heading L (SE) across vast wheat fields, with the Santuario di Picciano visible on a distant hill now. After rain, this section is exceptionally muddy and the following gently descending kilometres are challenging

At a cross lane by a minor **gas installation** (**24km**), turn R and climb steadily towards the quiet hamlet of **Picciano B** (**26.2km**). Picciano B was one of the satellite towns constructed for the inhabitants of Matera after it was evacuated in the 1950s (see 'Matera' box in the Introduction). Turn L before the houses onto a road – watch out for traffic! – in descent below Monte Castiglione, before a stiff climb the rest of the way to the monastery **Santuario di Picciano** (440m, **30.3km**).

SANTUARIO DI PICCIANO
LOCAL REP: MARIALAURA, TEL 327 7084471
STAMP: THE SANTUARIO (ON THE MAIN WALL FACING YOU)
The monastery and its community of Benedictine monks only provide accommodation for religious guests. Walkers stay at Masseria La Fiorita; it's 7km away and they pick you up from the Santuario and bring you back the morning after. Call them beforehand.

STAGE 7
Santuario di Picciano to Matera

Start	Santuario di Picciano
Finish	Duomo, Matera
Time	7hr 30min (alternative 4hr)
Distance	29.7km (alternative 16km)
Total ascent	530m (alternative 300m)
Total descent	570m (alternative 340m)
Difficulty	Moderately hard
Percentage paved	60% (alternative 95%)

While this stage means an extended walk, there are plenty of rewarding aspects such as the lake and the vast views, not to mention the glorious finale as you arrive in Matera at last!

Should it look too long, by all means take the shorter alternative described below. It mostly goes through built-up areas, including the satellite settlements specially designed for the residents of Matera.

Note: The second half of this stage gets muddy if wet; a small stream also needs fording (on the alternative route too) – be prepared to take off your shoes and socks if necessary.

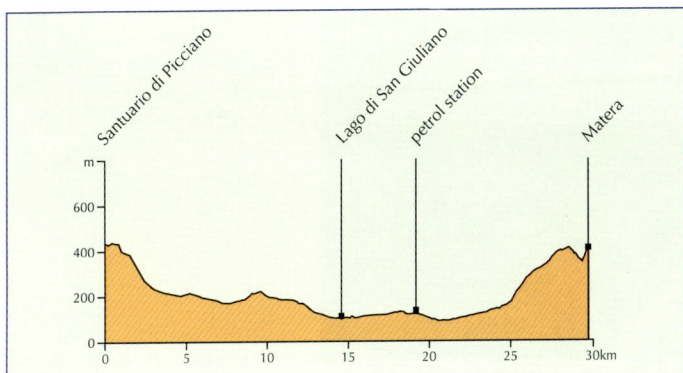

From Santuario di Picciano head straight across the parking area and follow the road downhill. Turn R after 1km and continue in descent to cross another road (**3km**). The shorter alternative breaks off here: see 'Variant route' below. Walk straight ahead and under a main road (**5km**), then onwards S to another road where a quick L then R sees you on a lane (**7km**) through cultivated land and some olive groves. This joins up with a scenic surfaced minor road SE all the way to **Lago di San Giuliano** (**14km**).

In 2006, a **fossilised whale** over 20m long, the largest of its kind in the whole of the Mediterranean, was found in the Lago di San Giuliano. Nicknamed Giuliana, she can be admired in the Archaeological Museum at Matera.

Take the shoreline path to well-placed picnic tables. Continue SE beyond the lake, walking above a deep ravine and the Bradano River, which is spanned by a disused **railway bridge**. Keep on until the VP takes you L to join a road before veering R

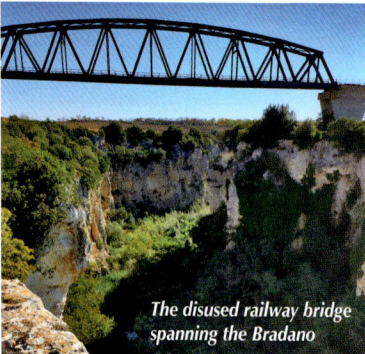

The disused railway bridge spanning the Bradano

70

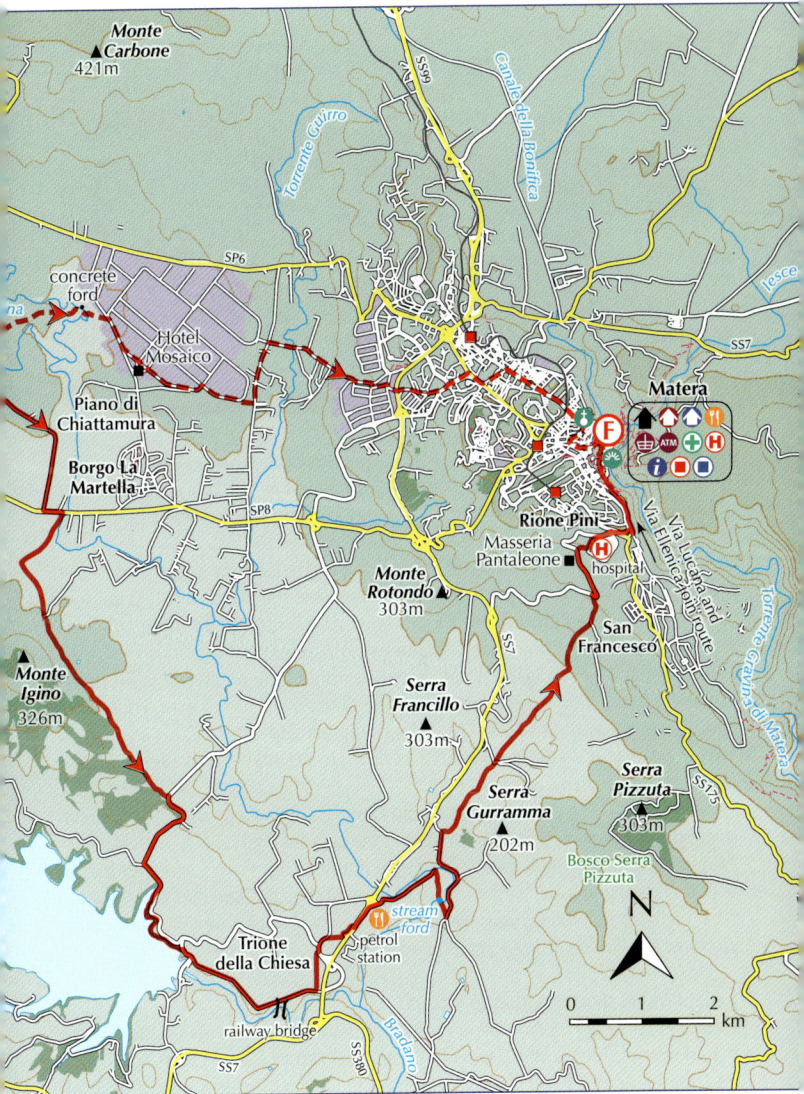

The breathtaking arrival in Matera

to a **petrol station** (**18.5km**, refreshments). Pass under the road and walk parallel to it then down a narrow, grassy lane to **ford a stream** (**20.5km**). Up the other side, take a sharp L (N) to a T-junction – go R for a long lane across rolling wheat fields past a farm or two.

Up at a busy road (**26.3km**), turn R around a hairpin and shortly after **Masseria Pantaleone** branch R up a path alongside the **hospital** (**27.5km**). Join the road again then go under a roundabout. At the next small roundabout go R then immediately L onto **Via Casalnuovo**. About 500m along, don't miss the fork R for the *Chiese rupestri* route. You're led out to the breathtaking lip of the yawning gorge, with Matera spread out ahead of your amazed eyes. Follow the paved stepped way past rock dwellings, lookouts and cafés, taking your time. The VP bears L to Via Bruno Buozzi and down to the superb **belvedere** near the **church of San Pietro Caveoso**.

Take the street L past I Tre Portali into Rione Pianelle then swing L and R onto stepped **Via Muro**, heading steeply uphill through the marvellous ancient town. At the top, a short way L sees you emerge into the surprisingly spacious piazza with the soaring Duomo (cathedral) of **Matera** (400m, **29.7km**) and the VP's gratifying conclusion. Finding your way around Matera is not a simple affair so allow plenty of time to locate your accommodation.

Variant route: shorter option to Matera

From Santuario di Picciano head straight across the parking area and follow tarmac downhill. Turn R after 1km and continue down to a road (**3km**), where you go L then R across fields then L on a gravel lane. This crosses a small river via a

concrete ford then climbs briefly to meet a road (**6.5km**). Turn R, but keep on the left-hand parallel road lined with industrial buildings, curving L (SE). Keep straight on past **Hotel Mosaico** (**7km**) then grain silos and a radio mast to a roundabout (**8.2km**).

Fork R in descent, continuing straight ahead at a large green building onto a gravel track (**8.7km**). Soon turn L onto tarmac, then at the top of a rise go R at a crossroads (**9.8km**). Descend through olive groves then climb steeply up Via della Tecnica to an intersection (**11.2km**). Now go L up past factories. At the next intersection (**11.4km**) turn R then L on Via della Scienza.

At a roundabout, branch slightly R, crossing the **SS7** on a flyover and heading up through suburban developments to a complex intersection with shops (**12.5km**). Keep on through a roundabout. These roads are very busy so use crossings where possible.

At the next junction turn L at the roundabout onto Via Alessandro Manzoni, then R onto broad tree-lined avenue **Via Nazionale** (**13.9km**). Keep to the L of a small park (**14.8km**) then head down **Via Stigliani** and R onto Via San Biagio. This leads past the church of San Giovanni Battista and into spacious **Piazza Vittorio Veneto**. Keep to the L of the Banco di Napoli building and follow the old paved streets upwards (Via delle Beccherie and **Via Duomo**) with superb views, to arrive at the Duomo of **Matera** (400m, **16km**).

MATERA 🔺 ⬤ ⬤ 🍴 ⊕ ᴀᴛᴍ ⊕ Ⓗ 🛈 ⬛ ⬛

LOCAL REP: ANTONIO, TEL 328 6481954

STAMP: STATIO PEREGRINORUM, VICO III CASALNUOVO (TESTIMONIUM TOO); LE LUCANE, VIA BECCHERIE 13

Volumes can be written about this unique rock town made up of labyrinthine *rione* (districts) known as the Sassi (stones), its buildings both below and above ground. Overlooking a dramatic canyon and spread over adjacent outcrops, Matera is punctuated with churches and belltowers, which make handy landmarks as orientation can be confusing to say the least. The word 'maze' does not do it justice.

Dozens of *chiese rupestri* (cave churches), many frescoed, dot the surrounds. A guided walk around town is highly recommended; don't miss the mammoth underground cistern known as the 'Palombaro lungo' beneath Piazza Vittorio Veneto.

A visit to the opposite side of the yawning canyon is a must. A low Himalayan-style bridge leads across the bottom, and good paths climb up the steep flanks exploring cave chapels, dwellings and plenty more. Naturally this is an excellent photo vantage point for Matera.

See the Introduction for more.

Murgecchia

Strada del Belvedere

San Pietro Caveoso

Via Ellenica and Lucana
join route

Via Cappuccini

Via Casalnuovo

Via Lucana

Rione
Pini

Via Peuceta

Duomo

Via Muro

Via Fiorentini

Via Ridola

SP10

Via Peuceta Sud Matera

(H)

(F)

Via Stigliani

Via Lucana

Via Levi

Via Castello

Via Antonio Persio

Via Lanera

Viale Carlo

Piazza
V. Veneto

Via Grotti

Via Nazionale

Via Peuceta variant route

Via Lupo Protospata

3

Matera
Centrale

Matera

Via Saragat

Via Antonio Passarelli Gattini

Viale Europa

Cimitero

Parco
Macamarda

Via Dante Alighieri

Via Timmari

Rione Spine
Bianche

Viale
Europa

Via dei Normanni

San Giacomo
Nuovo

N

0.5 km

0

Matera – Via Peuceta

1. B&B Fiorentini
2. B&B Mikasa
3. Hotel Albergo Roma
4. Ostello dei Sassi

VIA ELLENICA

Start	Brindisi
Finish	Matera
Time	14 days (77hr)
Distance	287.6km
Ascent	4865m
Descent	4425m
Getting to Brindisi	You can easily get to Brindisi from all over Europe by train (www.trenitalia.com), long-distance Flixbus (www.flixbus.it) or plane (https://brindisi.airports.aeroportidipuglia.it); if arriving by plane, take the bus from the airport to the city (www.stpbrindisi.it). Ferries galore from Albania, Greece and Montenegro dock here.
Note	The Cammino Materano and Via Ellenica are abbreviated throughout the route description as CM and VE.

The Cammino Materano organisation has split the Via Ellenica into two distinct sections: the opening six stages from Brindisi to Alberobello are known as the Via Ellenica *variante*, then the remaining eight stages to Matera are the main Via Ellenica. However, for the purpose of this guide, it is described as a single ongoing route, with the stages numbered 1–14.

Getting to the Cammino start

From Brindisi Centrale railway station, walk NE along **Corso Umberto I** through **Piazza Cairoli** and its park, and onwards to blend L onto **Corso Garibaldi**. This leads straight to the waterfront, where you turn L into the pleasant pedestrian area with its cafés and restaurants. The **Scalinata Virgilio** is third L. Around 30min is sufficient.

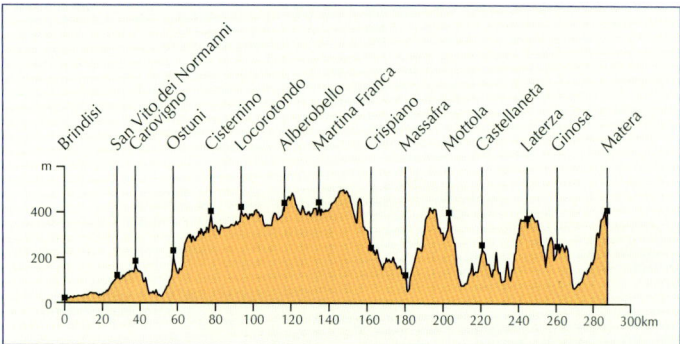

BRINDISI

S

1

San Vito
dei Normanni

2

3 Carovigno

4 Ostuni

Cisternino

Locorotondo

5

6 8 Martina
Franca

Crispiano

7 Alberobello

9

10 Massafra

Mottola

11

Palagiano

TARANTO

Monopoli

Polignano
a Mare

Torre a Mare

BARI

Bitetto

Molfetta

Santeramo
in Colle

12 Palagianello

Castellaneta

13 Laterza

14 Ginosa

MATERA

F

Montescaglioso

Adriatic Sea

Ionian Sea

N

km

20

10

0

Brindisi

Scalinata
Virgilio

Piazza Duomo

Accademia
degli Erranti
(CM office)

Via Tarantini

Via Castello

Tempietto
San Giovanni
al Sepolcro

Carmine
Piazza
Cairoli

Corso Garibaldi

Via Lata

Via del Mare

Via Taranto

Corso Umberto

Brindisi
Centrale

Via Tor Pisana

Strada per Patri

Strada per Patri

Canale Patri

Viale Arno

Via del Mare

Airport

Via Vespucci

Largo Vespucci

Via America

Via Ettore Circiello

Via Nicola Brandi

Via Provinciale per San
Vito

Strada Comunale Pitachi

Via Tor Pisana

Via Sicilia

Viale Commenda

Via Germanico

Via Pace brindisi

Viale San Giov

Via Appia

Via Lucio Strabone

Via Arione

Via Fiume

Via Trento

Via Matta

Via Aprilia

Via Sabaudia

Via Pontinia

Via Cappuccini

Via Ellenica

Via Cappuccini

Strada per Lo Spada

Parco Del
Cillarese

Strada Statale 16 Adriatica   SS16

SS16

N

0.5 km

0

Brindisi

1 B&B Mare Nostrum   2 Hotel Barsotti   3 B&B Dionisio

•••••• route to Cammino start

78

You walk through the old heart of Brindisi

BRINDISI ⌂ ⌂ 🍴 ⛴ ATM ➕ Ⓗ ❶ ▣ ▣

LOCAL REP: ANTONIO, TEL 388 113 0368

STAMP: ACCADEMIA DEGLI ERRANTI, VIA GIOVANNI TARANTINI 35

Once a strategic point of departure/arrival for traders, armies and pilgrims heading across the Mediterranean and for the Holy Land, the harbour of Brindisi (accent on the first syllable) hums with activity, embracing fishing boats as well as the vehicle and passenger ferries that ply the 'entrance' to the Adriatic and over to the coast of Albania, Greece and Montenegro.

The rich history of this attractive city stretches back to ancient Greek and Roman times, via Barbarians, Longobards, Byzantines, Normans, Turks, Venetians, Spaniards, Austrians…and this is reflected in its layout, architecture and monuments. Do find time to explore the old town – don't miss the Tempietto San Giovanni al Sepolcro, a replica of the one in Jerusalem.

Brindisi's inviting waterfront is dotted with cafés. Curiously, the city name derives from 'deer head', for the layout of the harbour, and this features on the crest – and the Cammino stamp.

STAGE 1

Brindisi to San Vito dei Normanni

Start	Scalinata Virgilio, Brindisi
Finish	Piazza Carducci, San Vito dei Normanni
Time	6hr
Distance	27.8km
Total ascent	165m
Total descent	60m
Difficulty	Easy
Percentage paved	65%

The VE starts on Brindisi's attractive waterfront at the marvellous Scalinata Virgilio, named after the ancient Roman poet who lived nearby. The broad staircase is topped with two massive marble columns (2nd–3rd centuries AD), marking the end of the strategic Roman Via Appia.

Stage 1 bids farewell to delightful Brindisi and heads out into rural Puglia. The walking is mostly flat, and while the stage is rather long, it helps you get into a cammino rhythm.

Note: At the time of writing there were no waymarks on this stage, so follow instructions and GPX.

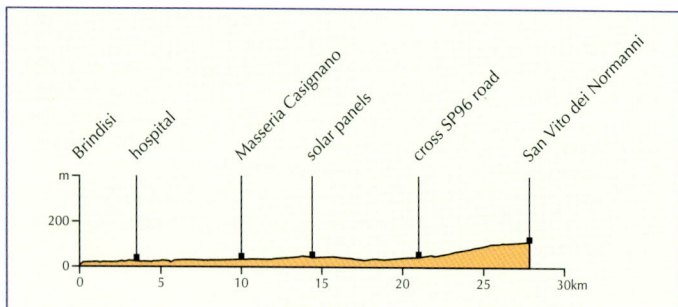

Walk up the Scalinata Virgilio in Brindisi (15m) to the columns at the top and follow paved Via Colonne through to **Piazza Duomo** with its beautiful cathedral. Continue straight ahead past elegant 14th-century Loggia Balsamo on **Via G Tarantini**, past the **Accademia degli Erranti** (CM office). Dogleg R and L onto Via Madonna della Neve then **Via del Castello**, which gives you a glimpse of the imposing castle. At traffic lights, keep L to cross the **railway line** and pick up Via Osanna. Where it forks, go R on **Via Cappuccini** and under the **SS16 motorway** (**3km**).

After the **hospital**, fork R onto a rough road dipping under the **railway** and up to vineyards. Soon a lane branches R, rounds a bend to cross a stream and rambles W through fields. At a road (**8km**) keep L to wind turbines then follow a road R to an avenue of pines and **Masseria Casignano** (**10km**). At its rear, take a rough lane leading towards the railway before bearing W to **solar panels** (**14km**) and grapevines. A stand of eucalypts precedes another series of roads and lanes, essentially heading NW past olive and almond trees.

At a shallow gully opposite farm buildings, follow the weaving way to the **SP96 road** (**21km**). More quiet country lanes lead in and out as the route heads W now and rejoins the **SP96** (**26.6km**). Walk along the pavement, then branch L on Corso Leonardo Leo through to a pleasant square with a towering obelisk bearing the town's patron San Vito. Continue through the pedestrian zone past the castle

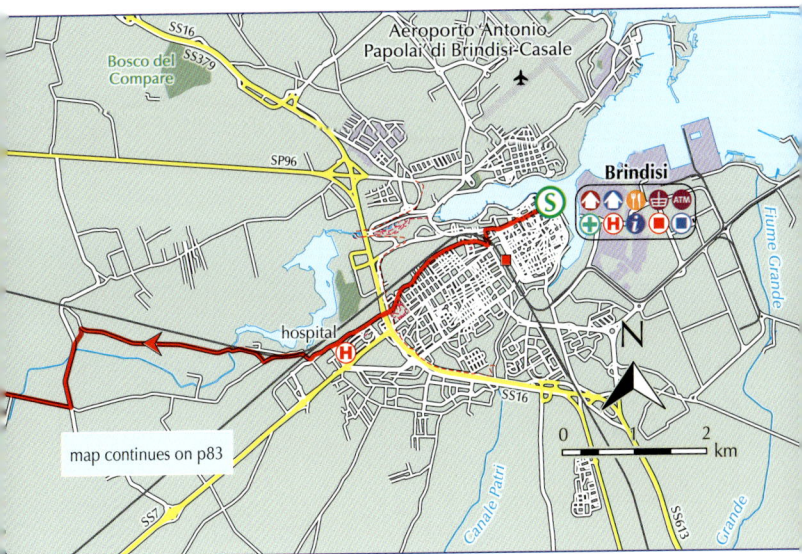

map continues on p83

The Scalinata Virgilio overlooks the harbour at Brindisi

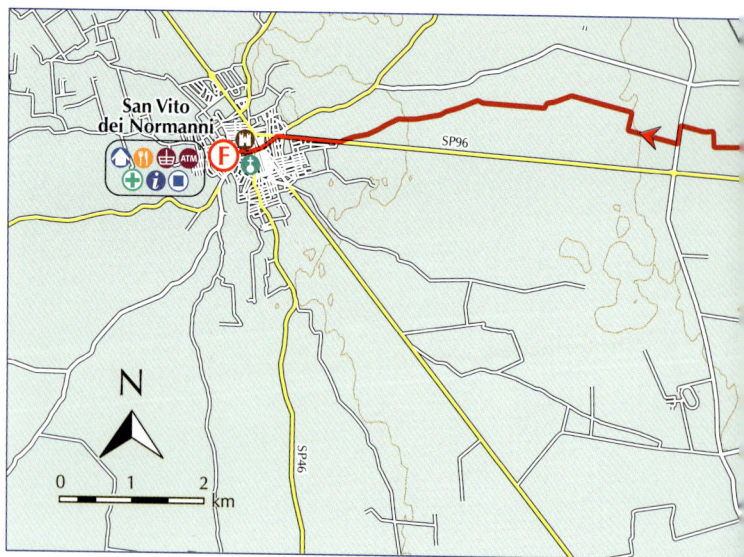

San Vito
dei Normanni

SP96

N

0   1   2 km

SP46

to the day's conclusion in spacious Piazza Carducci, with cafés, the Municipio and tourist information office of **San Vito dei Normanni** (108m, **27.8km**).

SAN VITO DEI NORMANNI ⟳ 🍴 ⊕ ATM ✚ 𝒊 ▣

LOCAL REP: ASK ACCOMMODATION PROVIDER
STAMP: ASK ACCOMMODATION PROVIDER

A laid-back town with grids of narrow streets lined with single-storey houses but also a castle. The history of San Vito dei Normanni is chequered to say the least. Possibly founded in medieval times by Croatians fleeing from Saracens, it became a hunting base for the Normans. It was later sacked by the Venetians, no less, before being encompassed by the Republic of Naples. The town was the birthplace of talented Baroque composer Leonardo Leo, and today is home to a renowned mandolin school.

VALLE D'ITRIA

The VE spends a lot of time in the broad Valle d'Itria, which spells olive trees galore. It was named in honour of the Madonna Odegitria, from the Greek for 'guide', as it is reputed to point wayfarers in the right direction.

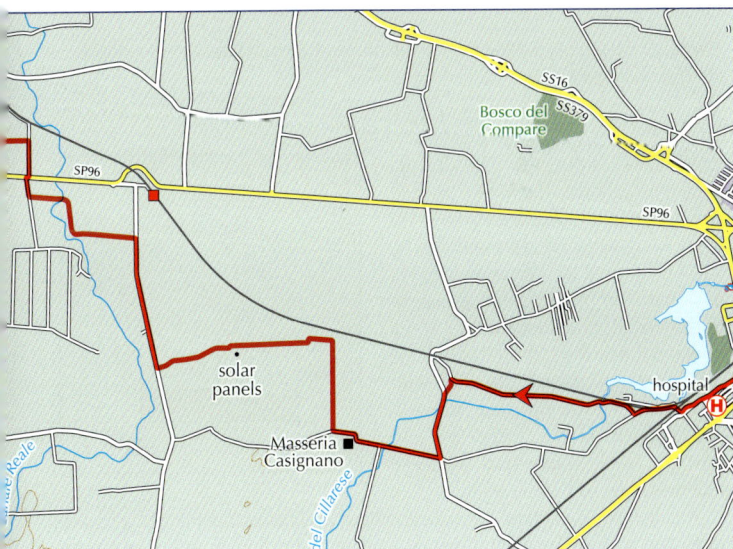

STAGE 2

San Vito dei Normanni to Carovigno

Start	Piazza Carducci, San Vito dei Normanni
Finish	Castello Dentice di Frasso, Carovigno
Time	3hr
Distance	9.8km
Total ascent	90m
Total descent	30m
Difficulty	Easy
Percentage paved	80%

Relatively short and sweet, this stage has a high percentage of paved surface but these are mostly minor roads through olives groves, woods and rural properties.

Note: At the time of writing there were no waymarks on this stage, so follow instructions and GPX.

From Piazza Carducci in San Vito dei Normanni, walk past the Municipio and tourist information office then L down Via Regina Margherita. At gates and a park, go R then around the corner to take Via de Gasperi NW past houses and vegetable gardens. After a sports centre and a roundabout near flats, the VE passes the **Carabinieri** (police) premises. Stick with the winding narrowing road; where it forks, keep R on the 'Percorso Ciclo Turistico' (cycle route) past scattered properties lined with stone walls.

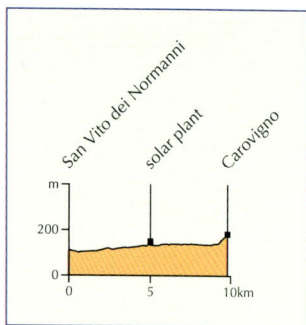

   A lane takes over (**4km**) through woodland and fields, dipping through olive groves and past a **solar plant** (**5km**). At a nearby T-junction, branch L on tarmac

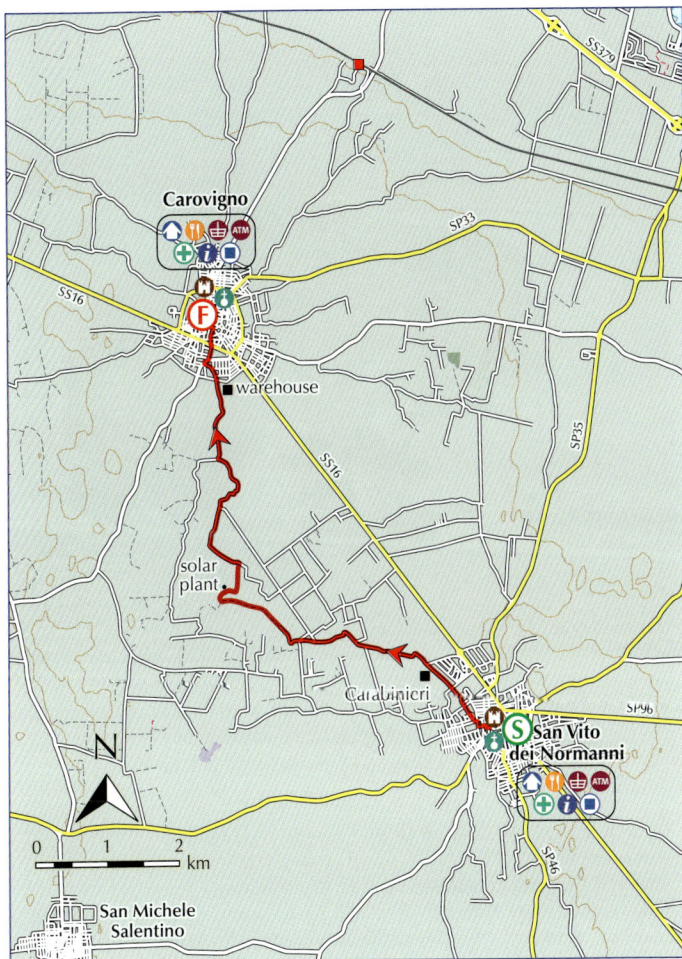

and stick with this rural way N, in the company of the first traditional conical *trulli* buildings of the VE. See 'Trullo' box in Via Peuceta, Stage 2. Carovigno comes into sight on a hill ahead. After a **warehouse** (**8.6km**), cross straight over a road then at a school go R to a modern church. Keep straight up the hill into the pleasant old

A curious old farm building

part of town with its historic buildings. At the top, keep L under arches following signs for the *castello* (castle), winding up to the entrance of Castello Dentice di Frasso in **Carovigno** (172m, **9.8km**) and the conclusion of Stage 2.

CAROVIGNO ⬡ 🍴 🏛 🅰 ✚ ⓘ ◉

LOCAL REP: NONE

STAMP: TOURIST INFO, CORSO EMANUELE 25, TEL 393 0834404

This pleasant white town with beautifully paved streets has a host of cafés and eateries, as well as a visitable castle (www.castellodicarovigno.it). The name Carovigno probably derives from the ancient Greek for 'fruitful', on account of its fertile land.

STAGE 3
Carovigno to Ostuni

Start	Castello Dentice di Frasso, Carovigno
Finish	Cattedrale Santa Maria Assunta, Ostuni
Time	5hr
Distance	20.3km
Total ascent	290m
Total descent	250m
Difficulty	Easy
Percentage paved	55%

A combination of farm tracks and stretches of road make up this longish but enjoyable stage as the VE loops north, well waymarked. Grove after grove of ancient olive trees is traversed, reputedly some of the oldest in the whole of Puglia, hundreds of years old. Gnarled, bent, sculpted by wind and water, trained by man. The day's reward is a true delight for the eyes – your arrival in the marvellous 'white city' of Ostuni, although its tourist crowds come as a bit of a shock after the quiet countryside.

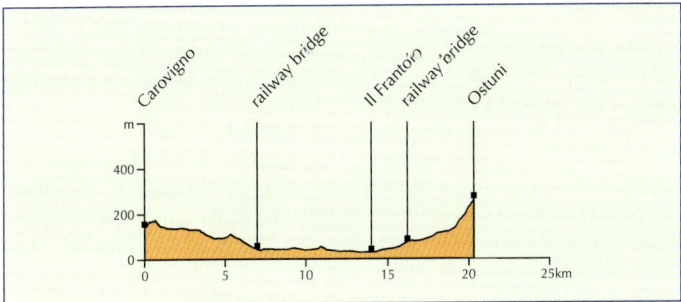

From the Castello Dentice di Frasso in Carovigno, the VE quickly reaches a huge church and turns R downhill, flanking a park then the monumental cemetery. Cross over the main road then through the **Parco delle Colonne** on a wide avenue of cypresses. Minor roads then meander mostly NW and N in the company of olive and almond trees and the odd trullo. You walk a short stretch in common

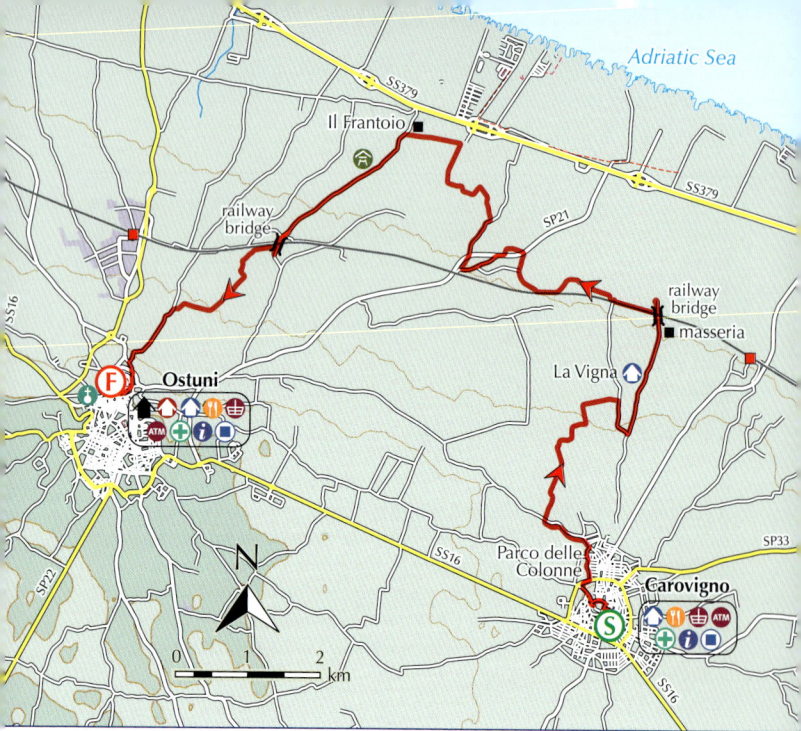

with the Via Francigena Sud, strolling downhill looking towards the distant sea, passing ⬡ **B&B La Vigna**. Next to a **masseria** farm, the road crosses a **railway bridge** (**7km**) and the VE doubles back L to follow the train line W.

Don't miss the lane L (**8km**) that cuts through fields before rejoining tarmac then crossing the busy **SP21 road** twice. As you approach the **railway** again near a bridge, fork R to soon cross the **SP21** again for a lovely unsurfaced way (**11km**). This follows a channel at first then winds through olive groves and fields and squeezes around a gate. As tall stone walls line the way, Ostuni, blinding white, appears in the distance. At **Il Frantoio** walled property (**14km**), pick up a narrow tarmac way L, SW now.

Further on is a **bench and info board** about the coastal dunes here. After recrossing the **bridged railway line**, loop R past ancient gnarled olive trees on a pleasant lane stroll. The VE eventually hits the tarmac (**18.5km**) and approaches the historic town of Ostuni. Take great care crossing the main road, keeping L to Via Francesco Vitale. This climbs past low cliffs and man-made bastions draped with caper plants. Cross a road and continue in the same direction. As you reach the town itself, don't miss the fork R under arches on a narrow alley crammed with restaurants and shops. Proceed uphill to the marvellous Romanesque Cattedrale Santa Maria Assunta, squashed into a tiny square in **Ostuni** (218m, **20.3km**).

OSTUNI 🔺 ⌂ ⌂ 🍴 🚊 🏧 ➕ 🛈 ◻

LOCAL REP: CONCETTA, TEL 338 5635008

STAMP: INFO POINT, CORSO MAZZINI 8, TEL 0831 1982471

Whitewashed Ostuni seems to grow out of the rock and is crammed with tiny houses and elegant palaces linked by narrow paved alleys. The town occupies a hilltop with a marvellous outlook over a vast expanse of olive trees all the way to the sea.

The patron saint is Sant'Oronzo, and his statue adorns a 20m Baroque column in the main square; he saved the town from the plague in 1656 and is celebrated year in year out on 25–27 August with a spectacular procession of statues and horse-borne knights in historical costumes. Another famous inhabitant was the Donna di Ostuni (woman of Ostuni), a pregnant 20-year-old who lived here 28,000 years ago. Her skeleton came to light in a cave in the 1900s.

Towards Ostuni (photo: LS)

STAGE 4

Ostuni to Cisternino

Start	Cattedrale Santa Maria Assunta, Ostuni
Finish	Piazza Vittorio Emanuele III, Cisternino
Time	5hr
Distance	19.8km
Total ascent	540m
Total descent	350m
Difficulty	Moderate
Percentage paved	60%

This lovely stage has plenty of variety, starting with paths and old lanes lined by well-kept drystone walls, as well as the usual stretches of road. The day is marked by constant ups and downs, but nothing difficult. Olive groves and woodland are the flavour of the day, and trulli are plentiful.

From Ostuni's Cattedrale Santa Maria Assunta, head downhill to Piazza della Libertà with its column bearing Sant'Oronzo. Go R and straight ahead in descent, following signs for the *stazione*. Then turn L on Via G Pisanelli and R down Via Specchia with its car parks. Go next R – signs for 'Ba-Le' – and over the main road (**0.7km**) onto what quickly turns into a stony lane. Keep your eyes peeled for waymarks for the many twists and turns. A minor road leads through **Parco Archeologico S Maria di Agnano** (**4km**) then the VE veers L (S) on a panoramic path enclosed by drystone walls. In the company of fig and carob trees, it climbs gently through old terracing and shrubs, emerging at the 17th-century **Santuario di Sant'Oronzo** (**5km**).

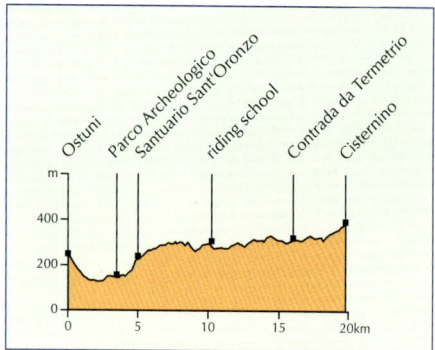

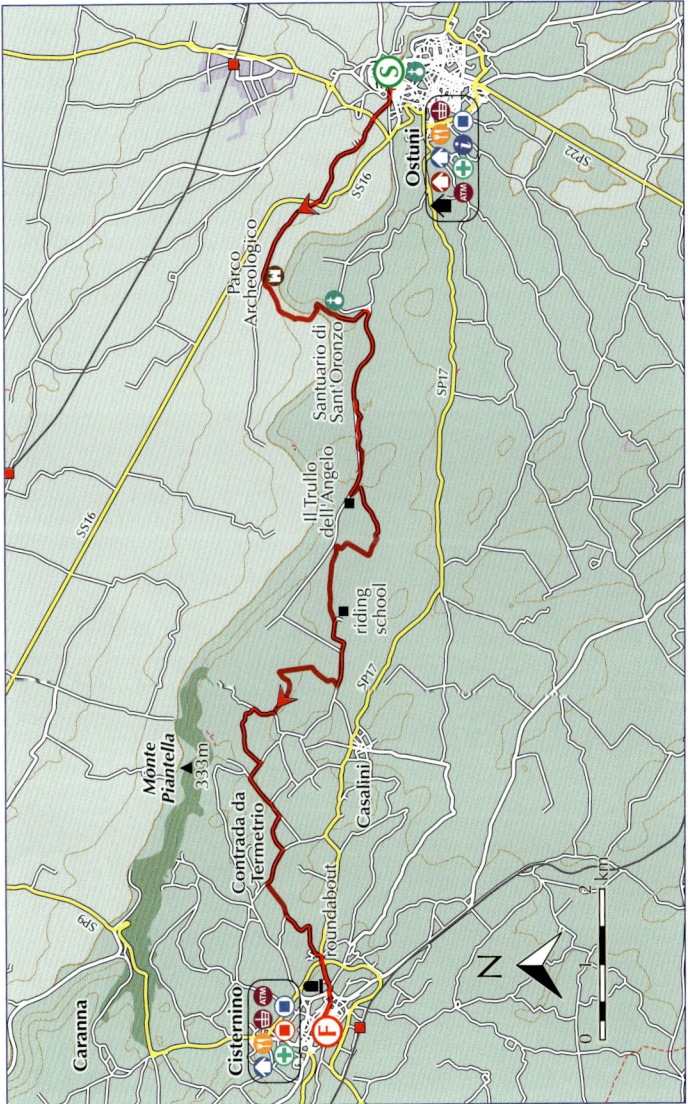

Ostuni

Parco Archeologico

Santuario di Sant'Oronzo

Il Trullo dell'Angelo

riding school

Casalini

Monte Piantella

333m

Contrada da Termetrio

Caranna

roundabout

Cisternino

N

km

Tarmac leads through woodland to the Strada dei Colli (keep R) – hopefully it won't be busy. As you reach houses, you're pointed L onto a handy series of lanes and paths. At **Il Trullo dell'Angelo** (**9km**) a minor road sharp L with ups and downs traverses countryside dotted with clusters of pointed trulli. Lanes ramble on through properties with olives galore, leading you onwards W through woodland to the **Red Water riding school** (**10.5km**).

Over a rise past scattered houses, fork R to leave the road (**12.5km**) for a series of lanes N through fields below Monte Piantella. Quiet roads take over, mostly W, to **Contrada da Termetrio** (**16km**) and its trulli. A picnic table (**17.2km**) marks the start of a path, before tarmac resumes to the main road and a roundabout (**18.5km**). Continue past the cemetery up Via Regina Margherita and Corso Umberto I, then branch L under arched Porta Piccenne into the *centro storico* and Piazza Vittorio Emanuele III with its stand-out clock tower. You've arrived in **Cisternino** (392m, **19.8km**).

Just some of today's curious trulli

The piazza and clock tower where the stage concludes

CISTERNINO ⬆ 🍴 🏧 ⊕ ◼ ◼

LOCAL REPS: ROBERTO, TEL 333 2311688; FRANCESCO, TEL 329 3851056

STAMP: PERCORSO ARCHEOLOGICO CHIESA DI SAN NICOLA, PIAZZA G GARIBALDI 11, TEL 380 5271525

A natural lookout over the vast Valle d'Itria, and listed as one of Italy's most beautiful villages, Cisternino was settled in the 9th century by coastal dwellers fleeing from pirates. The historic town centre is a delight, with its towers and maze of alleys and tiny house doors reached by narrow steep steps. 'A great masterpiece of architecture without architects' in the words of Hidenobu Jinnai, a modern Japanese architect who studied it in depth.

STAGE 5
Cisternino to Locorotondo

Start	Piazza Vittorio Emanuele III, Cisternino
Finish	Piazza Andrea Rodio, Locorotondo
Time	4hr 30min
Distance	16km
Total ascent	200m
Total descent	190m
Difficulty	Easy
Percentage paved	60%

Trulli galore is an understatement today; however, another great attraction is the Acquedotto Pugliese (AQP), the mammoth system of channels and pipes feeding water southwards (see 'Water' box in the Introduction for more information). The VE makes the most of an extended stretch of the raised pedestrian/cycle track that follows it. Another treat is pretty Locorotondo at the day's conclusion.

Leave Piazza Vittorio Emanuele III in Cisternino with the clock tower on your L, and head SW along Via Basiliani. As you exit the *centro storico* at Piazza Garibaldi with its war memorial and belvedere, go L along Via Manzoni but quickly leave it by taking the first R. Steps and ramps descend S to the **railway line**. Take a sharp L to a level crossing (**1km**) where you loop R and soon resume S again. A series of minor roads and lanes through fields lined with drystone walls wiggle S then W.

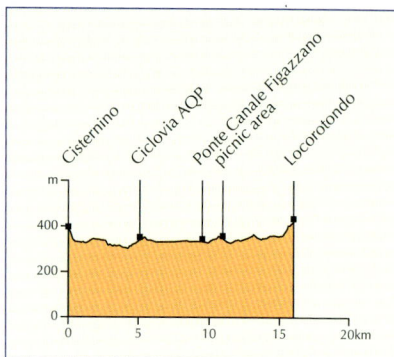

A giant sprawling Mediterranean oak tree precedes the trulli of **Contrada Fantese**, then the VE heads down to join the white gravel lane of the **Ciclovia dell'Acquedotto Pugliese** cycle track (**6km**). Lined by wooden railings, it goes unflinchingly NW in the company of almond orchards, vineyards and olive trees to a road crossing (**8km**, refreshments are available at a café 100m off L). Further on it drops below the railway line (**9km**) before crossing the marvellous arched **Ponte Canale Figazzano** (constructed 1906–15). Leave the AQP cycle track for a minor road, which becomes Via dei Trulli through Contrada di Agazzano to a picnic area (**11km**), where the AQP reappears briefly. Locorotondo comes into view, its domed church and belltowers feeling quite close.

Branch L (S) through **Contrada Tagaro** and on to join a main road at a **roundabout** (**14.5km**). Watching out for traffic, keep L through another roundabout then leave the road for a grassy lane up through lovely terraced vineyards. At the top, go L along panoramic Via Nardelli, skirting the edge of town to the park

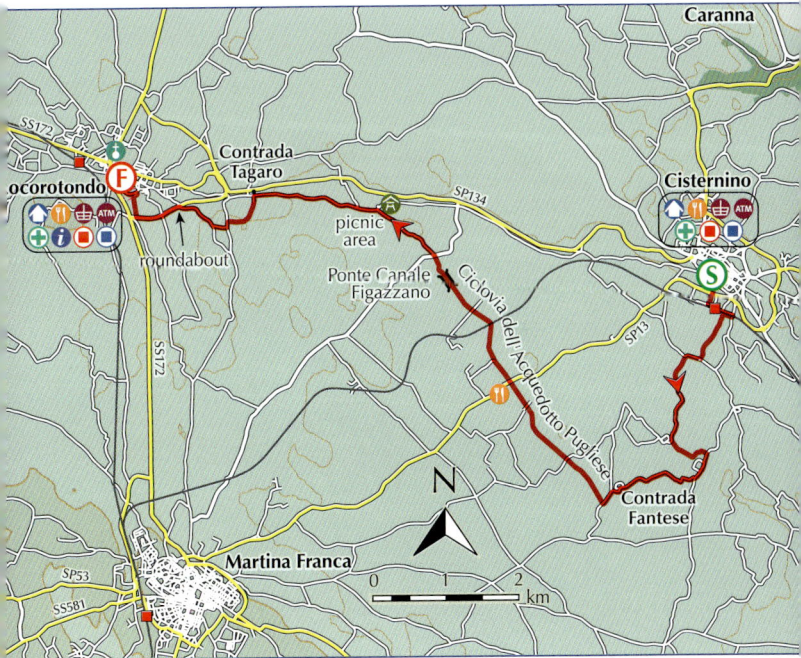

belvedere, then fork R under an arch into beautiful **Locorotondo** (410m, **16km**). Thread your way past the tourist information point and through to the cathedral in centrally located Piazza Andrea Rodio.

LOCOROTONDO ⬡ 🍴 ⛪ 🏧 ➕ ℹ️ 🟥 🔲

LOCAL REP: ANGELA, TEL 329 3824187

STAMP: INFO POINT, VIA MORELLI 24

Located in the midst of a flourishing wine-growing district whose terraces spill down around the town, attractive 'Locus rotundus' is an unusual circular ensemble of elegant Baroque palaces. Alongside are traditional multi-storeyed houses with sloping roofs, whose facades are plastered with lime, blindingly white. Reminiscent of slender Dutch houses, they are known as *cummerse* and feature the drystone construction technique.

The delightful approach to Locorotondo through vineyards

STAGE 6

Locorotondo to Alberobello

Start	Piazza Andrea Rodio, Locorotondo
Finish	Largo Martellotta, Alberobello
Time	6hr
Distance	23km
Total ascent	340m
Total descent	315m
Difficulty	Moderately hard
Percentage paved	50%

This stage of the VE does an enjoyable longish loop north from Locorotondo through rolling countryside before concluding at renowned Alberobello. En route it weaves its way in and out of small agricultural holdings with almonds, vineyards and a multitude of trulli. A long section of the AQP (see Stage 5) leads through woodland, with a wealth of Mediterranean shrubs and trees and welcome shade. On the whole it's peaceful and well signed.

Note: If you're tired, or tempted by the thought of spending extra time strolling around Alberobello, do consider the train from Locorotondo – it's a mere 10min trip, in contrast to 6hr on foot. The choice is yours.

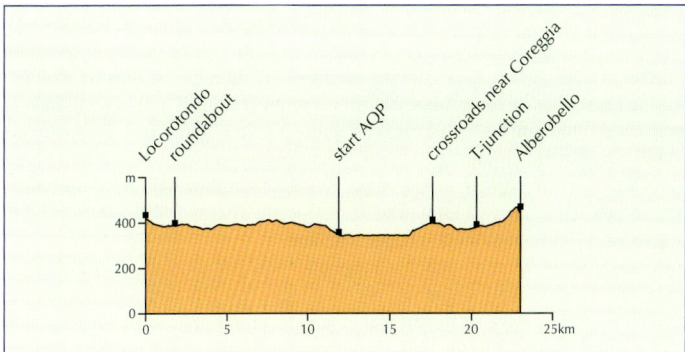

Alberobello comes as a real surprise!

Leave Piazza Andrea Rodio in Locorotondo and the old part of town. Turn down Corso 20 Settembre to an intersection with traffic lights and veer L on Via Alberobello. Continue to Via G Gentile (**1.1km**) then go R and take Via Balbo and Via Verdazzo. Cross straight over a roundabout (**1.8km**) in common with a cycle route through the countryside, dotted with farms and trulli, many beautifully restored. The quiet way takes many turnings so keep an eye on the GPX tracks as well as VE waymarks; sections of road are followed but never for long.

A stony lane descends to cross a road (**11.5km**) then proceeds NW through woodland to a bridge over a densely wooded chasm. You're on the **Acquedotto Pugliese** (AQP), which at this point runs mostly W through the **Bosco Calmerio**, a nature reserve. The route takes you over a series of bridges across small ravines and a road (**14.6km**) before proceeding through several gates for a short winding climb S to tarmac (**17km**); go L. Trulli reappear as you approach a crossroads (**17.7km**) near the village of **Coreggia**. (For ○, refreshments and shops, keep straight ahead to Coreggia itself.) The VE detours the village: follow waymarks R to a delightful L-shaped roadside **chapel** (**18.5km**).

Now a series of minor roads wander their way SW towards Alberobello, the gleaming sight of which urges you on. At a T-junction (**20.1km**) fork R and continue on via the **sewage treatment plant** then the railway line. Cross the main road and go easily up Via Turi then Via Verdi (which is back-to-back trulli), to emerge in a square with a fountain and a stunning belvedere. Go down the flight of steps and R along pedestrian avenue Largo Martellotta in **Alberobello** (428m, **23km**).

ALBEROBELLO ⭘ 🍴 🏛 🏧 ➕ ℹ 🔲 🔳

LOCAL REP: STELLA, TEL 338 9866964

STAMP: BAR BOSCO SELVA, VIA BOSCO SELVA

Founded relatively recently, namely late 14th century, as part of the Kingdom of Naples, the picturesque 'capital city of the trulli' has since 1996 had UNESCO World Heritage recognition for its unique buildings. Its veritable forest of trulli, numbering into the thousands, draws visitors from all over the world, who wander wide-eyed down the paved pedestrian streets, marvelling at the rows of fairy houses. (See 'Trulli' box in Via Peuceta, Stage 2.)

In the town name, 'albero' refers to an oak tree. Tourist facilities here are excellent.

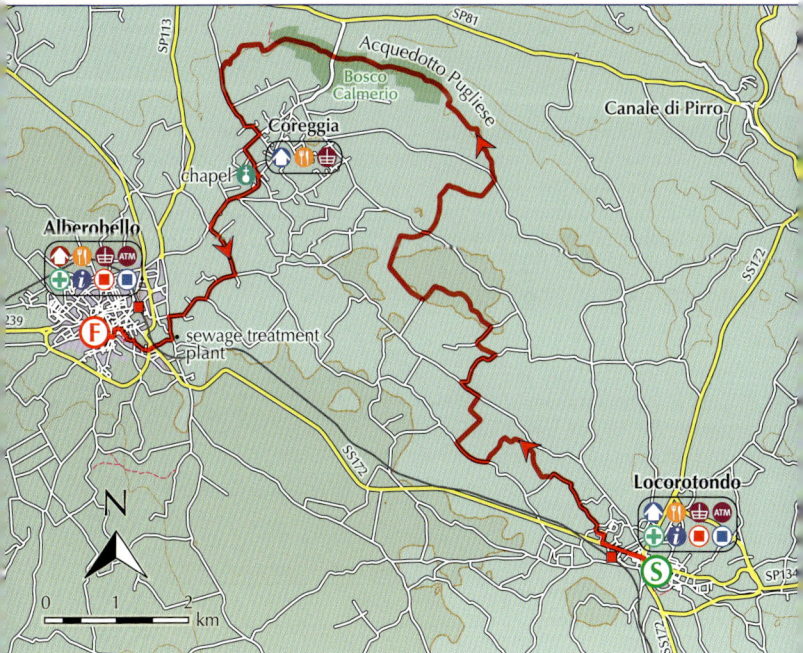

STAGE 7
Alberobello to Martina Franca

Start	Largo Martellotta, Alberobello
Finish	Piazza Plebiscito, Martina Franca
Time	5hr
Distance	18km
Total ascent	290m
Total descent	270m
Difficulty	Moderate
Percentage paved	55%

Signposting and waymarks are fairly plentiful on this stage. It's an easy-going day with plenty of shady woodland including well-established Bosco Selva, along with lovely paths through wheat fields, a blaze of bright flowers in early summer. There's no shortage of trulli en route either.

From Largo Martellotta in Alberobello, take Rione Monti and stepped Via Monte San Michele with its houses and boutiques. This leads to the church of San Antonio where you turn sharp L on Via Isonzo and head out to cross a main road at a roundabout. Continue S past a camping ground to a picnic area and drinking water (**1.3km**), where the VE enters **Bosco Selva**.

Clear paths lead through dappled woods of holm oak and lentisc. A road then leads S to a pleasant string of lanes and paths with the odd surfaced section. An abrupt L onto a road (**4km**) marks the start of a longish string of minor roads as you navigate past farms, wheat fields and livestock to a small settlement with a **school** and drinking water (**8.5km**).

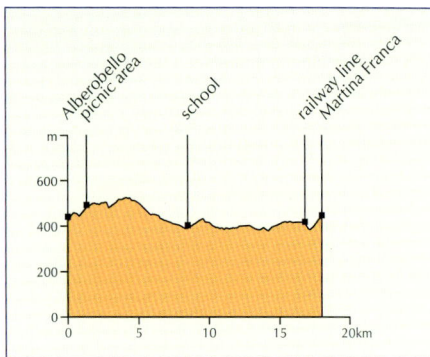

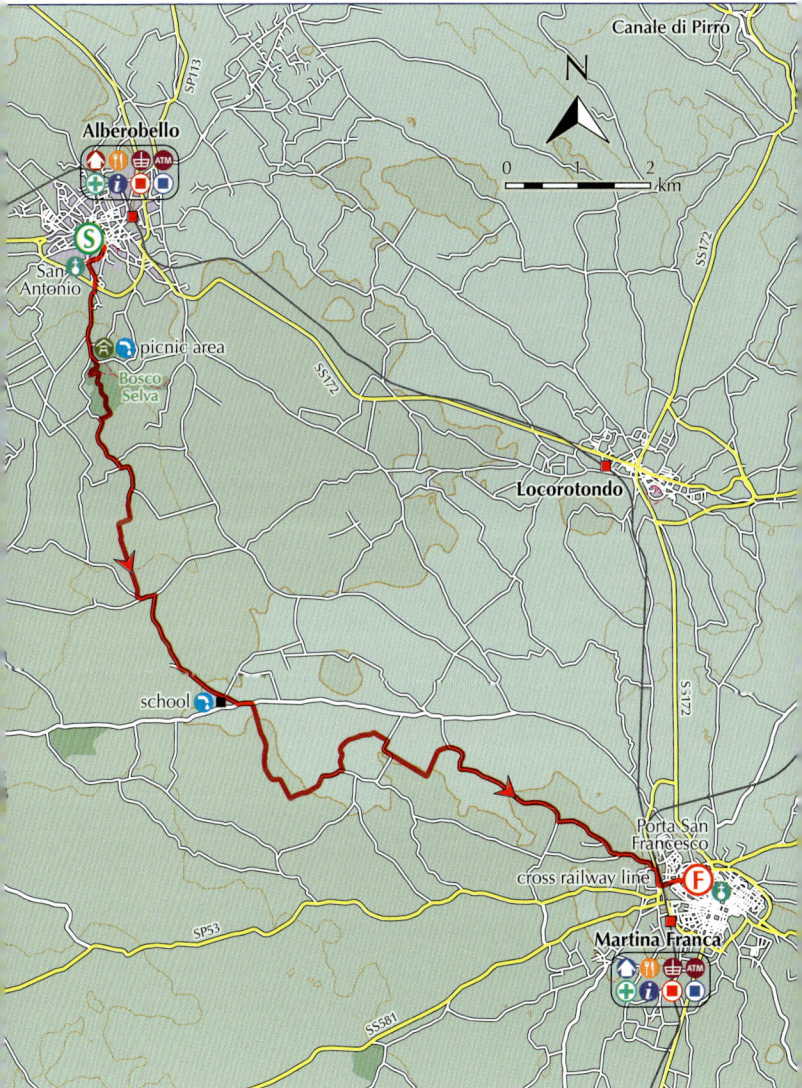

Canale di Pirro

N

0   1   2 km

Alberobello

San Antonio

picnic area

Bosco Selva

SS172

Locorotondo

SS172

school

SP53

SS581

Porta San Francesco

cross railway line

Martina Franca

SP113

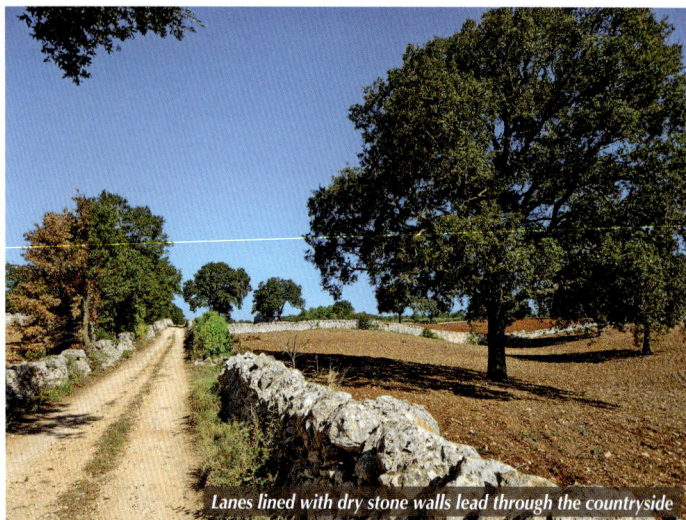
Lanes lined with dry stone walls lead through the countryside

Soon you're back to more lovely woodland lanes for a ramble past trulli, bearing E. At **13.2km** the VE joins a quiet road SE towards houses and downhill to a busy road. Cross the **railway line** (**17.4km**) for a short stroll uphill to Porta San Francesco and the entry into the heart of Martina Franca. Narrow paved Via Manzoni then Via Garibaldi with their tightly built houses lead into the densely populated inner precincts. After bustling semi-circular Piazza Maria Immacolata is the Basilica San Martino in Piazza Plebiscito of **Martina Franca** (431m, **18km**).

MARTINA FRANCA ⬡ 🍴 🚌 🏧 ➕ ℹ️ ⬛ ◻️
LOCAL REP: NUNZIO, TEL 335 1900130
STAMP: INFO POINT, PIAZZA XX SETTEMBRE, TEL 080 4116554
One of the first things to strike you on entering Martina Franca is the change in architecture – here churches and palaces are distinctly 1700s Baroque in style, especially ornate, and there are dozens of them! Don't miss the Palazzo Ducale, seat of the town council.

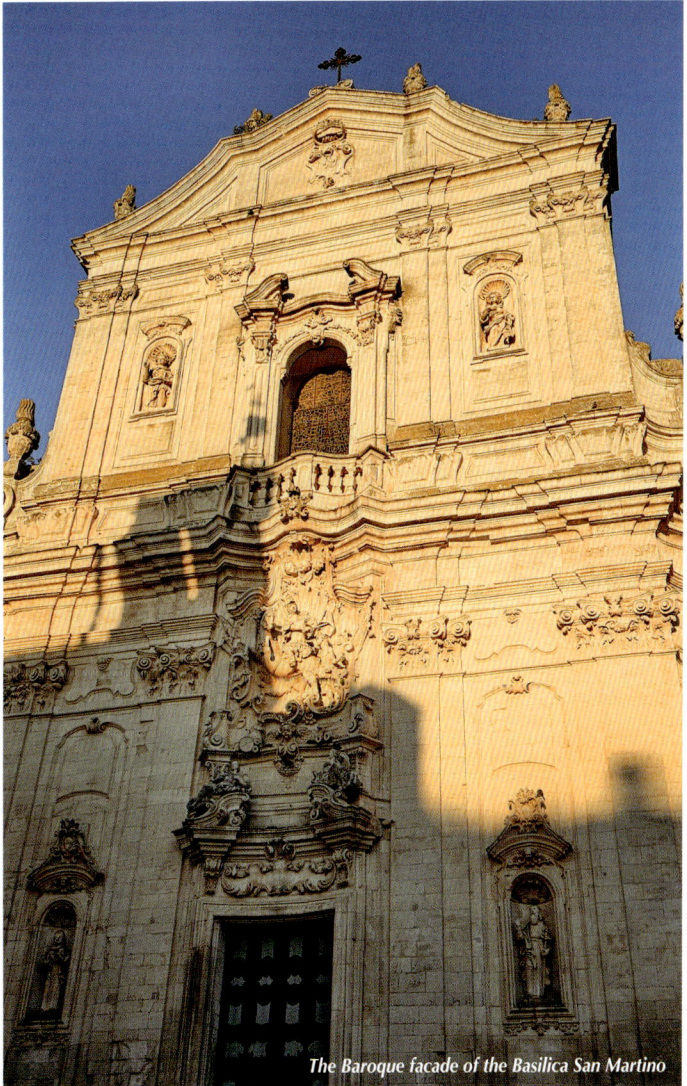

The Baroque facade of the Basilica San Martino

STAGE 8
Martina Franca to Crispiano

Start	Piazza Plebiscito, Martina Franca
Finish	Piazza Madonna della Neve, Crispiano
Time	8hr
Distance	27.4km
Total ascent	390m
Total descent	585m
Difficulty	Moderately hard
Percentage paved	55%

The opening section means a lot of tarmac, relentless at times, through open farmland with wheat and animals. A string of old rambling farms known as *masserie* are still operative. Halfway along the stage is Masseria Querciulo, run by 'Le Zie' (the aunts), who welcome walkers and conjure up delicious food (please leave a donation).

Afterwards, extensive woodland with shady Mediterranean oak trees dominates; one of Puglia's 'green lungs', Bosco delle Pianelle occupies a vast karstic dolina and features a multitude of wildflowers and orchids. Brigands rebelling against Italian state authorities took refuge here during the late 1800s unification. Despite the stage length, this is a satisfying day.

Note: It's possible to cut 10km off the stage by taking the CTP bus from Martina Franca (destination Massafra) and getting off at **Contrada Trasconi**. Then use your GPS to slot into the route.

Another variation is to overnight at the self-catering ⌂ Foresteria Bosco delle Pianelle, 5.4km before Crispiano.

Leave Piazza Plebiscito in Martina Franca, retracing your steps from Stage 7 down Via Manzoni and out through Porta San Francesco, and continuing down to cross the **railway line**. Keep R then L and away from town, soon parting ways with yesterday's route (**1.5km**).

A well-signed sequence of minor roads with stone walls and trulli, stretches of path and lanes zigzag their way SW mostly. You finally leave the tarmac (**8.4km**)

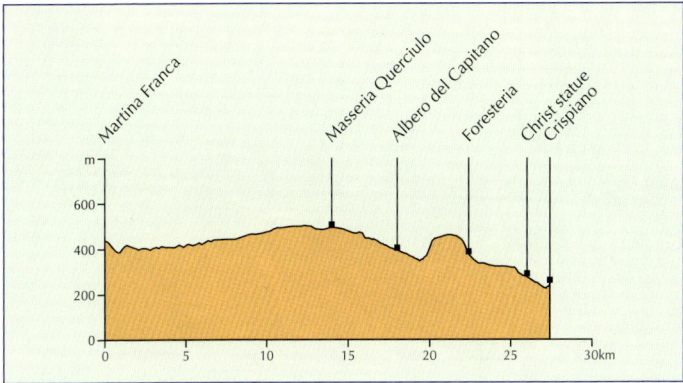

on a stony path through rock roses and the first of the shady woods, in common with the blue/red marked Rotta dei Due Mari route. A picnic table (**9.6km**) invites you for a rest. Lanes, paths and farm tracks alternate before quiet roads and a short detour to **Masseria Querciulo** farm for lunch or refreshments (**14km**).

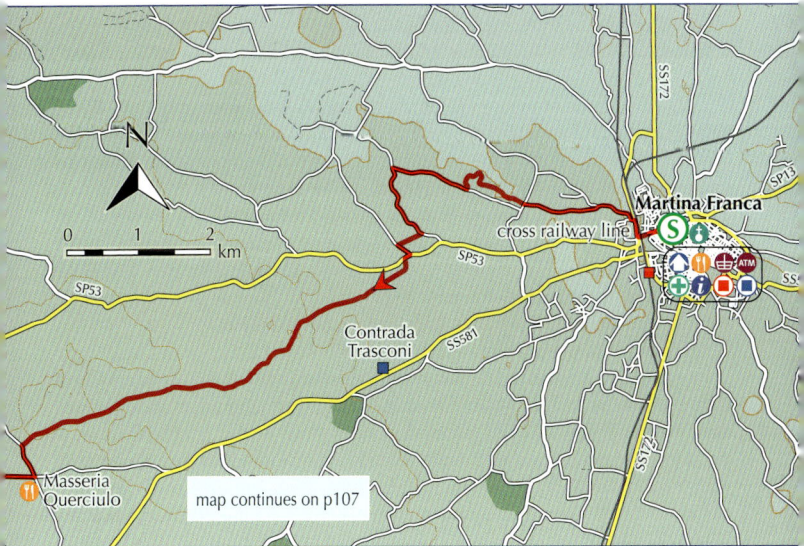

map continues on p107

Clear paths lead through Bosco delle Pianelle

After two lines of pylons (**15km**), a sign announces your entry into **Bosco delle Pianelle** and an enjoyable path lined with wooden railings. Follow signs carefully at the junctions as the way drops along the valley floor to the **Albero del Capitano**, a monumental holm oak (**18km**). By all means turn L on the lane over a rise – a shortcut. A disused road circles the hill then climbs steeply up rock terraces via clearings left by charcoal burners, to where a lane leads through a gate past military property. The shortcut rejoins the main route near the gate. Out at the main Martina Franca–Massafra road (**SS581**), cross to the car park with a picnic area and the ⬆ Foresteria Bosco delle Pianelle hostel (**22km**).

At the rear of the building, a path leads into woods then plunges past an old drinking trough. A series of lanes and minor roads proceed to the landmark **Christ statue** (**26km**), a great belvedere looking to your destination, Crispiano, as well as to the sparkling Gulf of Taranto and its steelworks. Tarmac continues down to the main road, where you go R then L onto Via Luigi Pirandello. At a **roundabout** with a park, turn L on Via Balilla then take the third flight of steps R up to the elongated white square Piazza Madonna della Neve and its church, in **Crispiano** (232m, **27.4km**).

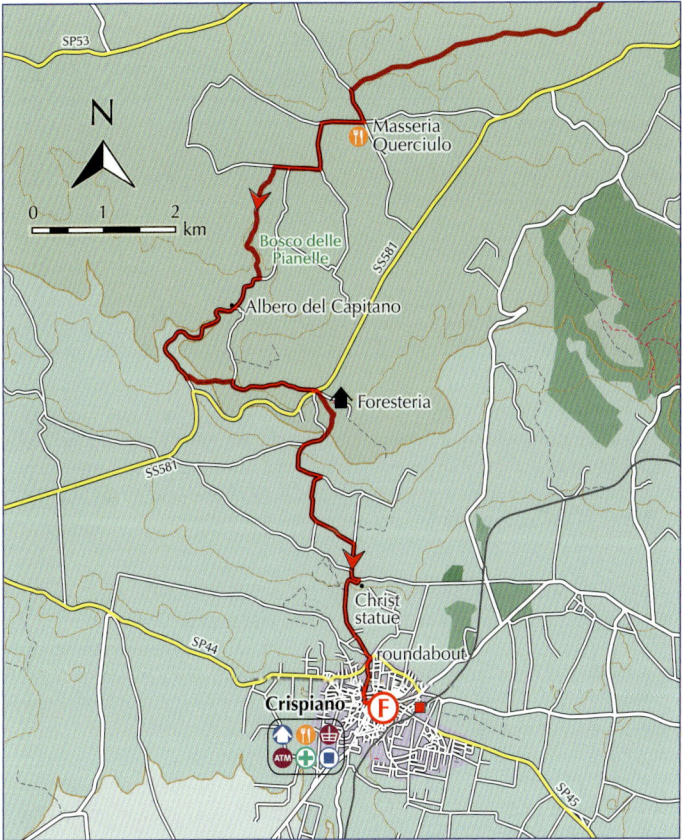

CRISPIANO ⌂ 🍴 🏛 ATM ✚ ▣

LOCAL REP: NONE

STAMP: IDEAL BAR, PIAZZA CENTRALE; INFO POINT, VIA ROMA 9

Low-key friendly Crispiano is known for its culinary speciality, grilled meat. In terms of geography, it's the dividing line between the Valle d'Itria and the Terra delle Gravine, the 'land of the ravines'.

STAGE 9
Crispiano to Massafra

Start	Piazza Madonna della Neve, Crispiano
Finish	Piazza Garibaldi, Massafra
Time	5hr
Distance	18km
Total ascent	165m
Total descent	325m
Difficulty	Moderate
Percentage paved	40%

Today marks the VE's entry into *gravina* territory, namely the yawning limestone ravines that cut through the rugged land, fanning out around the Gulf of Taranto. Thick with Mediterranean plants and shrubs and dotted with ancient cave dwellings and even frescoed rock chapels, these will be the flavour of each day for the VE's remaining stages to Matera.

Leave Piazza Madonna della Neve in Crispiano and head down the steps you came up yesterday. Go L along Via Balilla to touch on Piazza della Libertà, then initially straight ahead along a series of streets. Use the GPX tracks where there are no signs. Proceed S out of town on Via Monte Merlo through fields and olive trees.

Take a sharp R before a main road (**1.7km**) and follow a nice lane between stone walls where the VE is in common with Via dell'Angelo. After a gate you cross a field and enter a shallow valley, **Gravina Alezza**, with shady Mediterranean trees, scented herbs and birdsong as your companions. Towards the end, go under a road (**5.7km**) then an arched bridge and up steps to a road. This leads to a lane N through fields to a busy main road where you go L for 1km.

A clear path (**9km**) then proceeds due S over limestone rock grooved by the passage

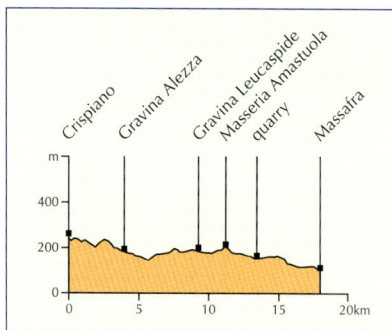

108

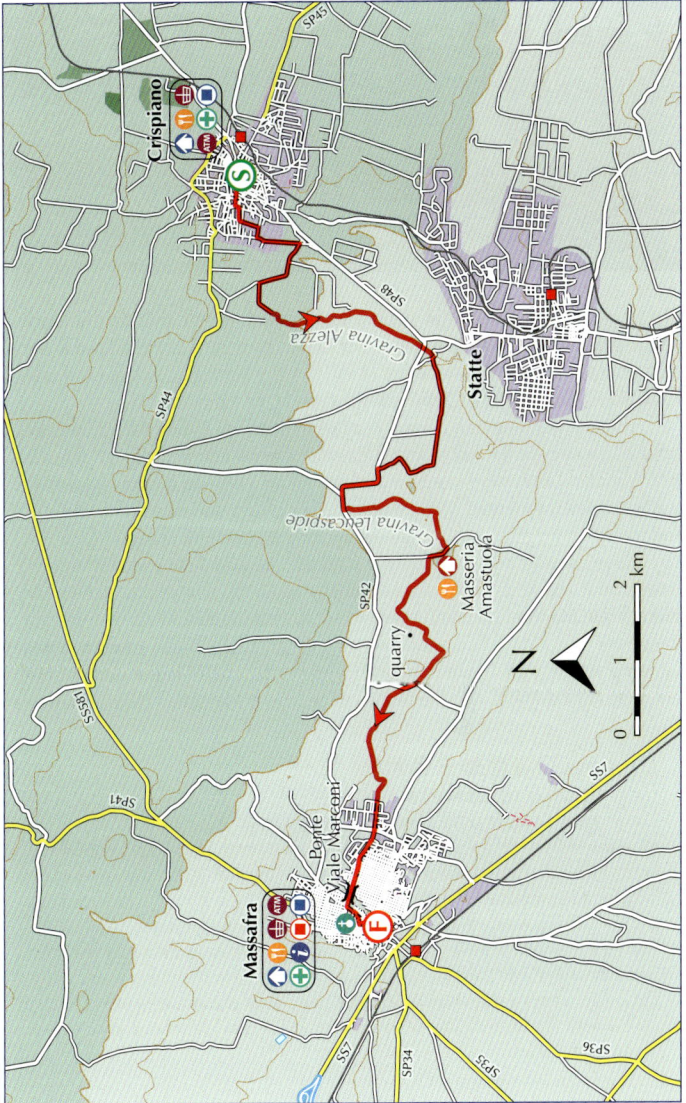

Crispiano

Statte

SP43

SP48

Gravina Alezza

Gravina Leucaspide

Masseria
Amastuola

quarry

SP42

SP44

SP44

SS581

SP41

Ponte

Viale Marconi

Massafra

SS7

SP34

SP35

SP36

SS7

N

km
2
1
0

A sea of vineyards surrounds Masseria Amastuola

of cartwheels and pitted with scallop fossils. Here the VE follows the **Gravina Leucaspide**, whose depths are thickly wooded. Where the way forks, keep R alongside what turns out to be a veritable ocean of vines belonging to hotel and winery ⬡ **Masseria Amastuola** (**11.2km**, refreshments) at the top of the hill.

From the buildings, an avenue of olive trees heads R then the VE branches L onto a lane, where the hill town of Massafra can be admired. Rough lanes lead into woodland with more fossils underfoot, before a **disused quarry** and a massive water conduit. More road, vines, trees, another quarry and wasteland, and all of a sudden you emerge on a cliff edge overlooking blocks of new flats.

Curve across a field and onto the road then keep straight ahead W through a roundabout and hosts of houses. You finally reach the marvellous arched bridge **Ponte Viale Marconi** (**17.5km**) over awesome Gravina San Marco. At the end of the bridge, go L on Via Dalmazia following waymarks to thread your way through winding streets. Pass the temple-like Chiesa di Lorenzo Martire and not far on enter Piazza Garibaldi with the tourist office. This is **Massafra** (110m, **18km**).

MASSAFRA ⬡ 🍴 🏛 ATM ➕ ⓘ ◼ ◼
LOCAL REP: MINO, TEL 339 3603823
STAMP: BAR ALLA TAZZA D'ORO, PIAZZA GARIBALDI 41/42

Massafra (the accent goes on the second syllable) stands on a knoll between two *gravine* (ravines). The laid-back town clusters around a castle that dates back to the 10th century, although evidence of settlement has been traced to Roman times; the Via Appia passed close by and rumour goes that the great general Hannibal had an encampment there. It was under Norman then Aragonese rule and flourished through the Renaissance period, as can be seen in its admirable buildings. Curiously, there's a settlement called Cicerone a short distance west of Massafra!

To visit the town's many decorated Byzantine rock churches and caves, ask at the tourist office.

STAGE 10

Massafra to Mottola

Start	Piazza Garibaldi, Massafra
Finish	Chiesa Madre, Mottola
Time	6hr 30min
Distance	23km
Total ascent	580m
Total descent	315m
Difficulty	Moderately hard
Percentage paved	55%

The VE makes a wide arc north today, touching on minor gravine and the flourishing woodland of Bosco di Sant'Antuono. Wide-reaching views are on the cards, along with fair amounts of ups and downs which make the stage rather tiring.

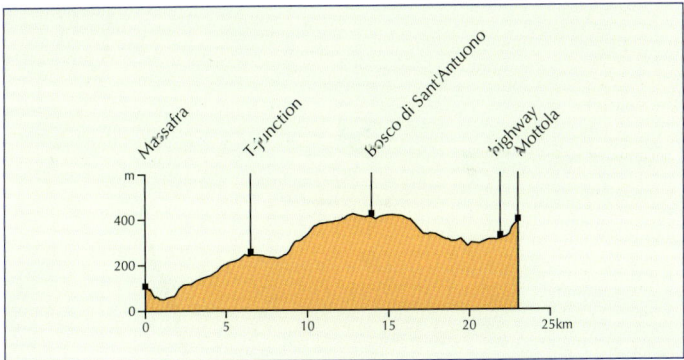

From Piazza Garibaldi in Massafra take the street on the opposite side of the square from the clock tower, then first R and L down flights of steps. Continue below the imposing castle to a junction and go R past a church. Waymarking leads onto a paved way close to an elaborately derelict church, Sant'Agostino. Keep L past **Frantoio Notaristefano** (an olive press with historic underground premises) and down to an intersection (**1.8km**) not far from the main road.

Here you're pointed up a country road signed for Camping La Stella, then next R (NE) past houses and into quiet olive groves punctuated with prickly pears and pines. Massafra and its domed church can be glimpsed. Asphalt alternates with rough stony lanes as you head along the side of a gravina (but the only way to see it is to detour over a field).

At a T-junction (**6.4km**) turn L to join a major road through farmland to where the VE peels off R (**7.9km**) into a field (ignore waymarks continuing along the road). A well-marked stony path ascends through waist-high rock roses and

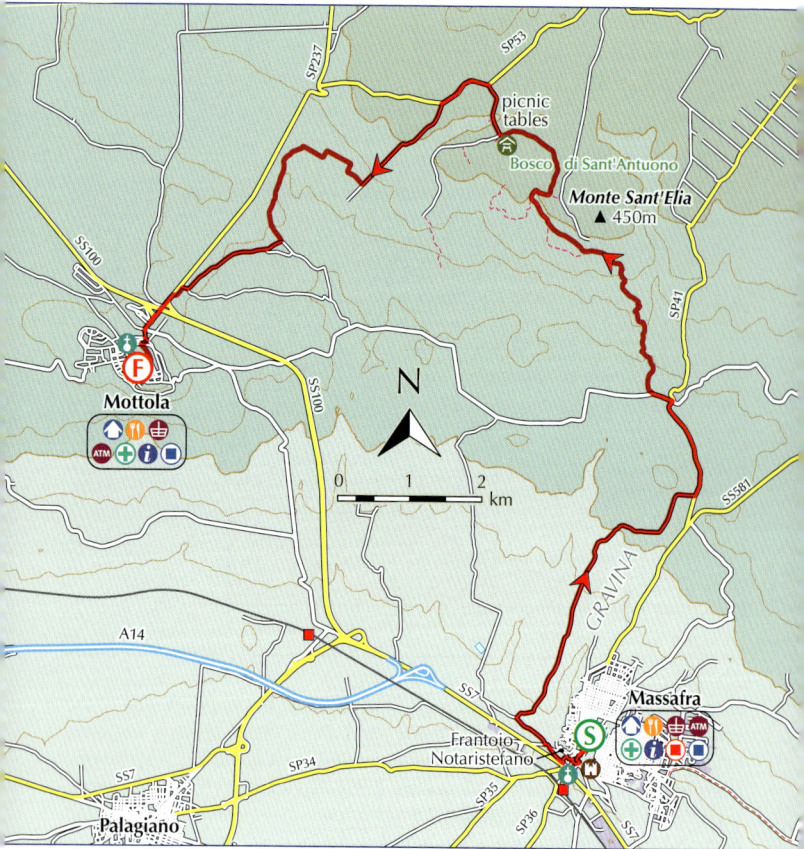

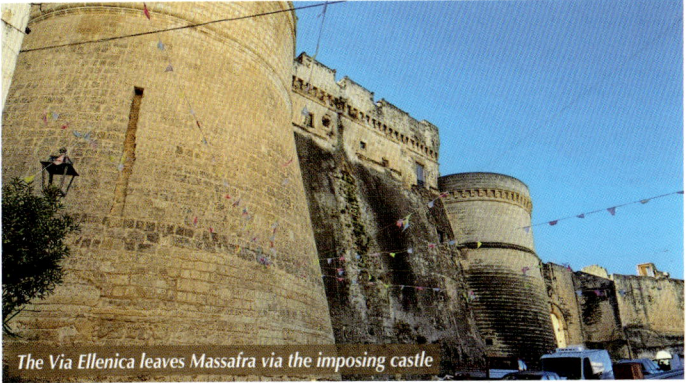
The Via Ellenica leaves Massafra via the imposing castle

scented maquis shrubs, and out to a lane. Steep at times, this winds up to the 419m mark. It's satisfying to be able to admire the views across the hills and plains to the sea. Cypress trees line the way through a World Wide Fund for Nature (WWF) reserve below Monte Sant'Elia, passing buildings. A rough lane and path lead on NW into the dense oak wood of **Bosco di Sant'Antuono** and picnic tables (**14.5km**).

Out at a road, turn L onto tarmac then lanes and a rocky path (**19km**) used by sheep, through wasteland dotted with squill and thorny bushes. The route approaches pylons then proceeds to a road over a **major highway** (**22km**). Keep straight ahead through a roundabout uphill on Via Turi, then take steps up to a park and the historic part of town. Branch L on panoramic Via Muraglia then Via Mazzini up to Chiesa Madre, the main church of **Mottola** (387m, **23km**), squeezed into a tiny square alongside a water tower.

MOTTOLA ⬡ 🍴 ⛪ 🏧 ➕ ℹ️ ⬛

LOCAL REP: GIANLUCA, 376 1598296

STAMP: BAR PIAZZA GRANDE, PIAZZA XX SETTEMBRE 7

Mottola (accent on the first syllable) is referred to as the 'spy of the Ionian' as it looks out over the Gulf of Taranto all the way to the Basilicata hills and the Sila massif in Calabria. It's a great place for sunsets. The whitewashed medieval town centre makes for a relaxing stroll and features an attractive elongated piazza where the locals hang out. Try the local *pinza*, a type of focaccia.

The village patron saint is St Thomas Becket, of all people, and two of his treasured relics are in the main church.

STAGE 11
Mottola to Castellaneta

Start	Chiesa Madre, Mottola
Finish	Cattedrale, Castellaneta
Time	5hr
Distance	17.5km
Total ascent	340m
Total descent	475m
Difficulty	Moderate
Percentage paved	45%

This is undeniably one of the most superb stages on the VE, with bags of history. Allow time out for detours to visit ancient underground settlements with frescoed rock chapels; you don't realise from the outside how extensive these are. Along the way, the VE also loops through Palagianello – which spells a refreshment stop – as well as plunging across a gravina. In addition, it follows the course of a former railway line, now converted into a walking/cycle track, featuring impressive bridges over deep ravines.

From Mottola's Chiesa Madre, follow Via Mazzini then Via Palagianello, heading downhill W towards the vast plain with its orderly rows of olive trees and views to the blue sea of the Gulf of Taranto. At 1.2km don't miss the fork L on a rough lane. A minor road curves past an old concrete **water tank** and a carob tree with benches (**2km**). Heading S, a stony lane looks across olive trees.

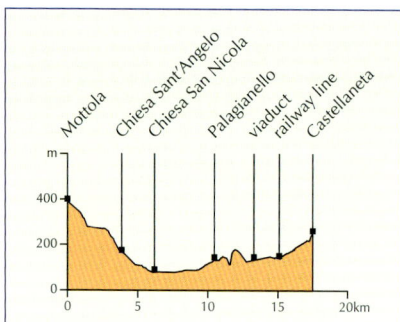

On a minor road opposite a huge masseria farm is a sprawling series of underground tufa cave premises draped with capers and fig trees, including the **Chiesa rupestre Sant'Angelo** (**3.8km**). A straight stretch of tarmac beckons due S

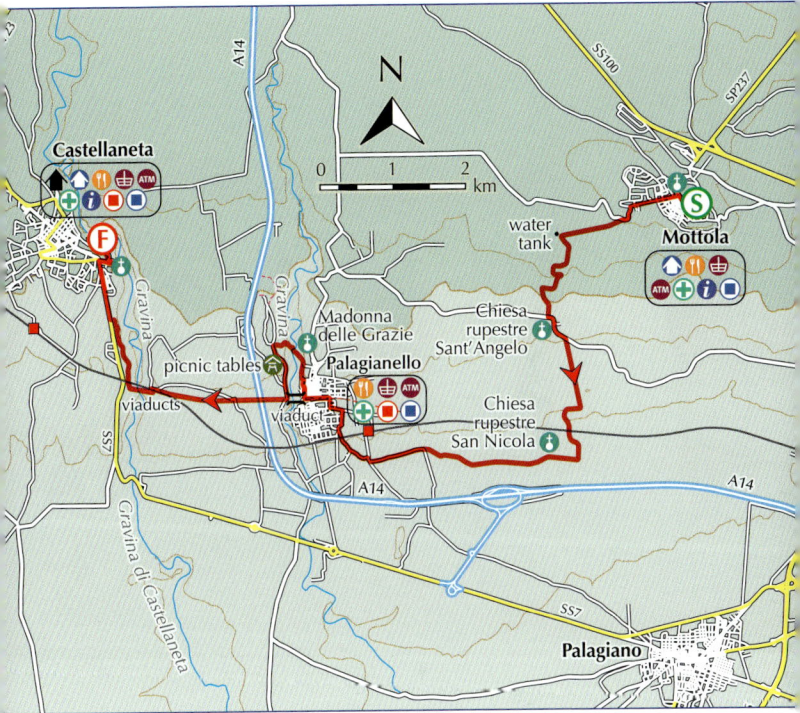

then dips under the **railway line (5.6km)** to a signed detour **(6.3km)** for the **Chiesa rupestre San Nicola**.

> Hidden on the edge of a gravina, the **Chiesa rupestre San Nicola** is well worth the 1km return detour to peek through bars and see its Byzantine-style frescoes. This 9th-century cave church is known as one of the 'Sistine chapels of southern Italy'.

Proceed due W on the unsurfaced road past citrus orchards and crops, then on tarmac under the railway and up into laid-back **Palagianello** (130m, **10.6km**, refreshments, shops, ATM, pharmacy, bus). You're pointed L onto a path parallel to Via Roma with its cafés; this is the former railway line, as testified by the locomotive at the far end!

115

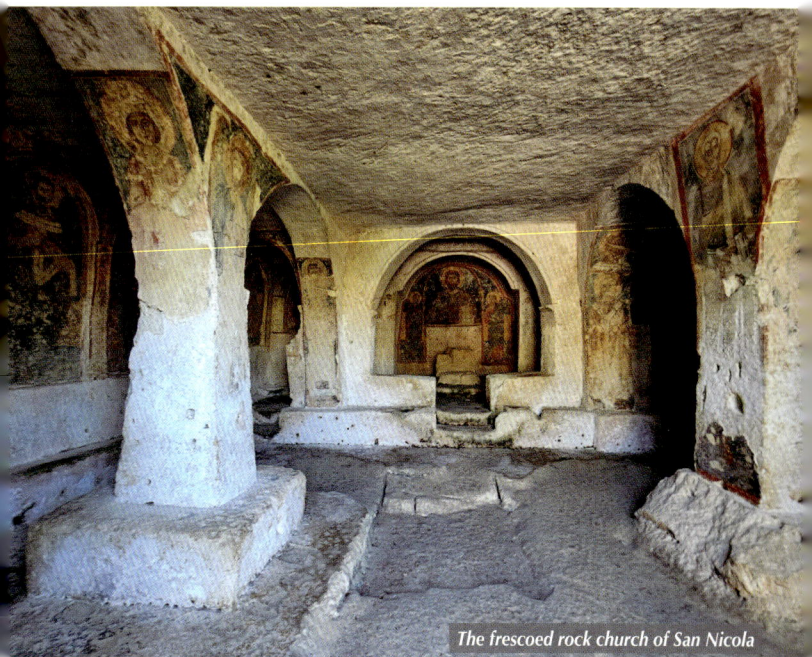
The frescoed rock church of San Nicola

SHORTCUT

You could continue straight ahead across the **viaduct** spanning the yawning gravina. Walkers must take this shortcut during or after heavy rain due to the risk of flooding in the ravine.

If not taking the shortcut, fork R on the VE and head up through Piazza de Gasperi, where you loop L around the church and castle, passing former dwellings, to the **Santuario della Madonna delle Grazie (11.4km)**. Drop down on steep stone-cut steps through terraces of prickly pear to the valley floor, past the water conduit, and puff steeply up the other side. Join a path to picnic tables and a car park, where a road leads S past a belvedere to the end of the **viaduct (13km)**. The shortcut joins back up with the main route here.

Turn sharp R on the former railway, now a cycle/pedestrian track, and proceed due W via olive groves and aromatic herbs before ducking under the modern
railway line (**15km**) over an old **viaduct** across an awesome gravina. The VE veers
R under the railway again on a marvellous path N hugging the edge of the ravine,
the town visible ahead. After a short stretch of main road, fork R on Via Capo
Orlando for the final uphill via a stately palace to the tiny square Piazza Federico
de Martino, housing the modest Cattedrale of **Castellaneta** (245m, **17.5km**).

CASTELLANETA 🔺 ⬠ 🍴 ⚖ 🏧 ➕ ⓘ ◼ ◻

LOCAL REP: FRANCESCO, TEL 327 4963021
STAMP: BAR ALMANI PLAZA, PIAZZA UMBERTO I N.43

Considered the centre of the Murge region, this delightful town with tight paved
streets derives its name from its late medieval castle; it was conquered by a long
series of lords. Get yourself to one of the signed belvederes to appreciate the
breathtaking dimensions of the gravina – 150m deep and 250m across at most. Try
to find time for a 'Castellaneta sotterranea' (underground) guided visit, as it opens
up a captivating albeit tenebrous world of labyrinthine corridors, stairs, stores
and old dwellings carved out of the rock (www.amicidellegravinedicastellaneta.it
or ask the local rep).

RUDOLPH VALENTINO

Yes! *The* one and only Valentino! The famous romantic silent movie actor of
Hollywood was born in Castellaneta in 1895 of a French mother and Italian
father. He went to the US in 1913 and quickly made his way to the film
studios, starring in memorable films such as *The Sheik* (1921) and *The Four
Horsemen of the Apocalypse* (1921). Incredibly, his birth year coincided
with the advent of silent films, while the year of his death, 1926, coincided
with their demise and the beginning of talking movies. He is fondly remem-
bered in his native town with a memorial and museum.

STAGE 12
Castellaneta to Laterza

Start	Cattedrale, Castellaneta
Finish	Piazza Plebiscito, Laterza
Time	7hr
Distance	24km
Total ascent	635m
Total descent	535m
Difficulty	Moderate
Percentage paved	40%

This is a remarkably varied stage with a great conclusion. The VE first heads through dense woodland which in the 1800s sheltered outlaws (*briganti*) but these days is home to wildlife, judging from the hoofprints. Then it follows the edge of the Parco Regionale Terra delle Gravine, with breathtaking outlooks over a rugged canyon.

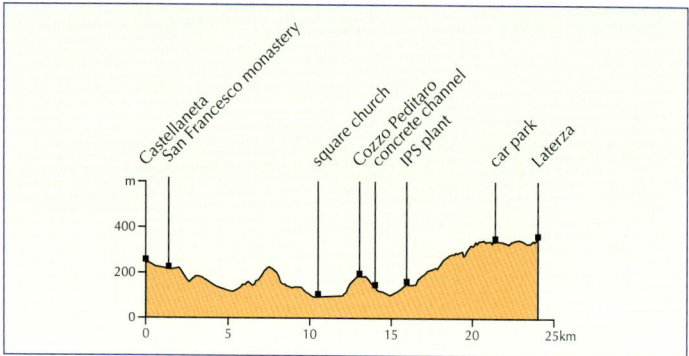

From Castellaneta's Cattedrale, walk out of the square W on Via Vittorio Emanuele then pick up Via San Francesco out of town, heading down the hill past the **San Francesco church/monastery** (**1.7km**, visitors welcome). Continuing in descent, a minor road leads S through agricultural land with olives and grapes and under a **viaduct** (**2.9km**). The tarmac continues to a lane branching L (**6km**), signed for

118

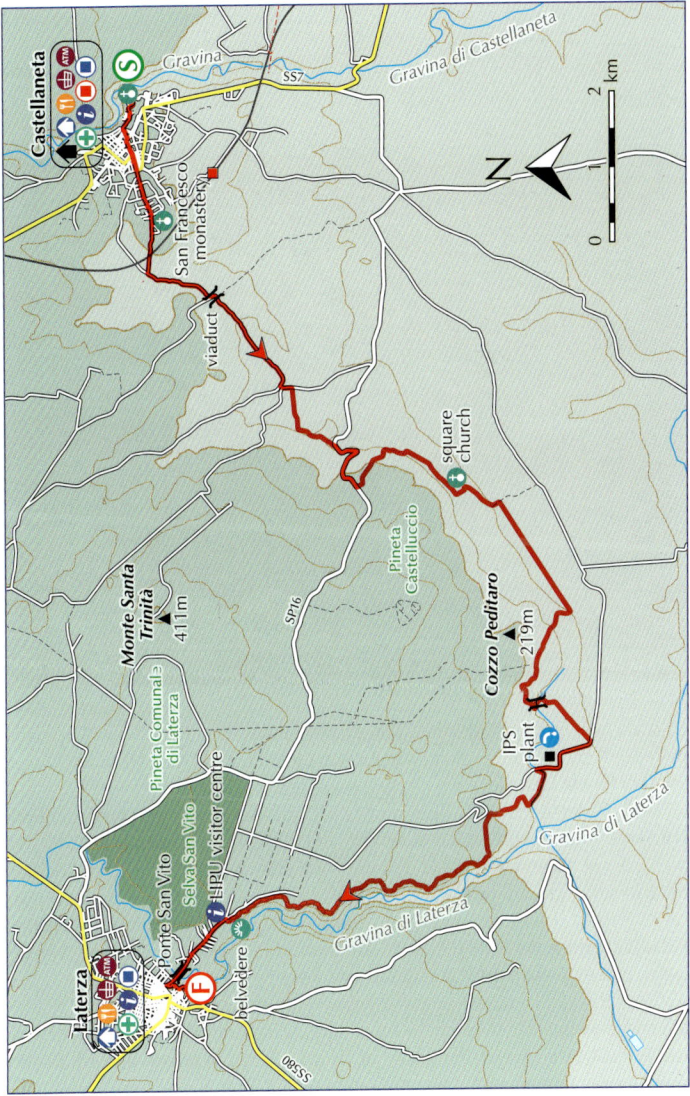

The Via Ellenica follows the edge of the Gravina di Laterza

Casa Vacanze Rodolfo Valentino. This quickly rejoins a road uphill. At **7km** a faint path peels off R through pine trees before crossing the road and proceeding S through **Pineta Castelluccio** with downs and ups.

The VE emerges at a field and leads you on to an old **square church** (**10.5km**). After a short stretch of tarmac, an enjoyable level track heads SW past orchards. At **12km** the VE forks R (NW) for a stiff climb below **Cozzo Peditaro** on arid stony ground past a water purification plant. Descend to cross a concrete channel (**14km**) and soon join a series of roads to the premises of **Impianto Potabilizzazione del Sinni** (IPS water treatment plant, **16km**). If you need drinking water, enter the main gates and turn R past the office to a tap.

Slightly uphill a track leads off L below a low tufa cliff and climbs on a stony path past old quarries to reach the lip of the gravina at last. The Gravina di Laterza is the most extensive in the whole of Europe, 12km in length and with sheer 200m cliffs. Now ensues a beautiful 7km section due N and mostly level. The path regales you with awesome views down into the plunging depths and out to where the gravina drops to the plain. Lentisc, rock roses, juniper and orchids accompany the weaving way along the jagged edge, with views of weathered towers and spires, and even pools of water on the canyon floor.

A fork detours L to a magnificent **belvedere** then you head out to a car park (**23.2km**). Turn L along the road to the **LIPU visitor centre** (Italian society for the protection of birds) then on to cross the impressive **Ponte San Vito** bridge over the canyon. The VE takes the first L, winding up the narrow streets of the town centre to Piazza Plebiscito and the massive Palazzo Marchesale in **Laterza** (362m, **24km**).

LATERZA ⬡ 🍴 🛏 ATM ➕ ❶ ◉

LOCAL REPS: LILIANA, TEL 348 2315005; NADIA, TEL 329 8278085

STAMP: INFO POINT, PALAZZO MARCHESALE; BAR BILICO, PIAZZA PLEBISCITO

Of the many drawcards for Laterza, its fragrant bread stands out. Its thick crust keeps the inside soft and edible days after baking; it was a staple for shepherds, who would be away from home for days on end. Each town district once had its own bakery.

Another rather different attraction is the excellent Museo della Maiolica (https://mumalaterza.it), showcasing elegant majolica pottery – at the peak of its splendour in the 1700s – with elegant jugs and platters exquisitely decorated in blue/white/yellow depicting scenes from mythology. Examples can be found in museums the world over.

Laterza appears on its perch

STAGE 13
Laterza to Ginosa

Start	Piazza Plebiscito, Laterza
Finish	Piazza Orologio, Ginosa
Time	4hr 30min
Distance	16km
Total ascent	255m
Total descent	345m
Difficulty	Moderate
Percentage paved	50%

Today's highlight comes at the end – Ginosa in its 'crater' riddled with ancient rock dwellings. But getting there is enjoyable too, traversing lovely countryside and woodland. The vast sparkling Gulf of Taranto is never far away, backed by the distant mountains of Calabria.

From Piazza Plebiscito in Laterza, take Via Chiesa then Via Concerie and pass the **medieval fountain** with its mask spouts. Keep L up a main road then soon L again on Via Cappuccini in gentle uphill S to the edge of a gravina past a monastery.

A lane takes over, skirting fields and olive groves, then a path through fields – watch waymarks and GPX. It joins tarmac (**2.7km**) for a long series of quiet minor roads, with wind turbines visible on the horizon. The farm **Masseria Ricciardi** (**8.1km**) has a *punto d'acqua* (drinking water). Where the road ends (**9.2km**), a lane with wooden railings leads in descent through pine woods before veering R (N) past a farm and over a hill with a **cross**, between olives and vineyards.

Gentle ascent on a woodland path in **Pineta Regina** passes fitness/exercise areas before the VE crosses a road to enter the premises of a large **farm** (**12.2km**, unchain the gate and rechain it behind you,

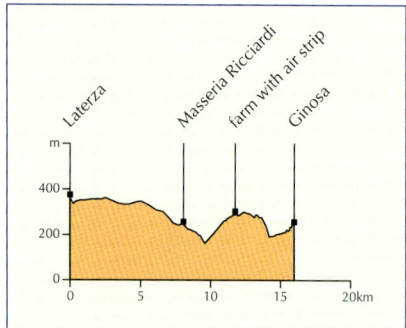

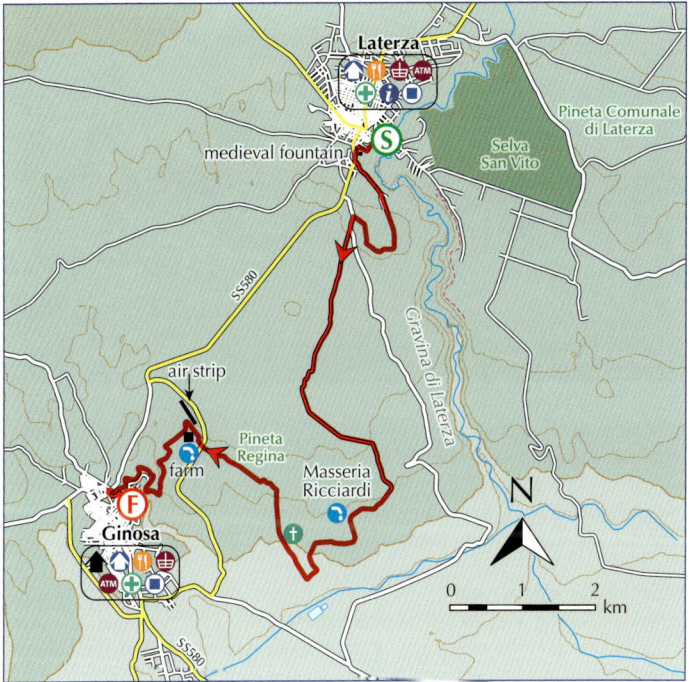

drinking water). Out the other side, near an **air strip**, the way drops into trees and flanks a field before huge yellow arrows lead SW through stone-ridden fields with low stone walls. Before you know it, the VE reaches the edge of the fascinating gravina housing old Ginosa and its multitudinous caves. A clear path lined with giant fennel drops via cave chapels to the valley floor (**14.2km**).

DETOUR TO RIONE RIVOLTA

When you reach the valley floor, by all means pop up the opposite side to visit fascinating Rione Rivolta with its underground cisterns, wine cellars and rock dwellings. Then either proceed to the old church with its scenic terrace and up via the castle to the stage conclusion at Piazza Orologio, or resume the official route (see below) along the stream bed.

The main track along the valley floor at Ginosa (photo: LS)

Official route

From the valley floor, the official VE follows the stream bed R. At the time of writing, it curved around the base of the old village to continue under a road bridge, before looping back along modern-day streets to the conclusion at Piazza Orologio in **Ginosa** (240m, **16km**).

Variant to the official route

Instead of staying with the official route all the way to the stage end, it is more enjoyable to follow the valley floor for about 800m as far as a modern flight of steps (resembling an amphitheatre) and branch L up to join Via Matrice. Continue up past a small church for steps to Corso Vittorio Emanuele, then turn L to Piazza Orologio.

GINOSA 🔺 ⬡ 🟠 ⬛ ᴬᵀᴹ ➕ ◾

LOCAL REP: LEONARDO, TEL 388 8971972
STAMP: RISTORANTE PIZZERIA PARISI, CORSO V EMANUELE 157

Possibly named after Janus, as the local population worshipped his cult, Ginosa is often referred to as Matera's little sister. The original village dating back to BC was abandoned bit by bit as the land became unstable and dangerous. An earthquake in 1857 caused widespread damage including cliff collapses, as did a flash flood in 2014.

Partly occupied until the 1950s, these days it has but a single inhabitant as everyone else lives in the upper town. Pier Paolo Pasolini's 1964 film *Il Vangelo Secondo Matteo* (*The Gospel According to St Matthew*) was filmed here, and he was even allowed to blow up a house to simulate an earthquake!

124

STAGE 14

Ginosa to Matera

Start	Piazza Orologio, Ginosa
Finish	Duomo, Matera
Time	6hr 30min
Distance	27km
Total ascent	535m
Total descent	380m
Difficulty	Moderate
Percentage paved	50%

The VE's concluding stage is characterised by a dramatic change in landscape – hilly country with clay, big fields and pale earth, not to mention vast views to the hill towns of Basilicata. The conclusion is magical Matera. Seeing is believing.

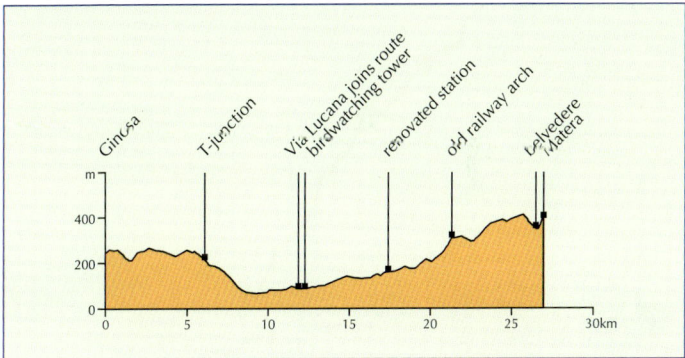

From Piazza Orologio in Ginosa, follow Corso Vittorio Emanuele SW, then go R on Via Roma and out of town to where a minor road forks R (**1km**). Proceed W at first past eucalypts and open fields in rolling countryside. A lane takes over (**5km**) below the knoll **Iazzo dei Tre Confini** (298m), with a view over to Montescaglioso on its outcrop.

Matera

Trasano

Serrone Trasanello
493m

412m

SS7

SS7

Torrente Gravina di Matera

Rione Pini

Monte Rotondo
303m

Via Peuceta joins route

San Francesco

Dimore all'Ofra

old railway arch

Lamaquacchiola

Serra Gurramma
202m

Serra Pizzuta
303m

Bosco Serra Pizzuta

SS175

Serra Marina
275m

Serrone di Alvino
509m

Serrone del Franzese
488m

Serra del Visciolo
389m

renovated station

Serra di Monsignore
351m

Iazzo dei Tre Confini
298m

Serra Maggiore
210m

Pianelle

birdwatching tower

Via Lucana joins route

Serra Sant'Angelo
289m

quarry

stream crossing

N

0   1   2
km

Montescaglioso

126

Down at a T-junction (**6.3km**) go L past an old **quarry** and scattered farms to cross a road (**8.7km**). In wet weather turn R here along the road to avoid problems with the stream crossing. After olive trees, a path loops across a stream bed colonised with prickly cocklebur plants then R along the edge of fields. Near a farm, the way is surfaced and leads out to a busy road (**11.3km**). Keeping an eye on traffic, walk carefully NW to a junction (**12.8km**) where the VE branches R, in common with the Via Lucana now. Keep straight ahead through an intersection then take the faint lane breaking off R. It runs parallel to the road, passing a quarry and **birdwatching tower** (**13.2km**).

The ensuing long straight stretch follows a former train line through tiny farms and the **Pianelle** *centro visite* onto a cycle track. Where the old railway is overgrown, the VE continues on tarmac towards vineyards. At a **renovated station building**, turn L along the main road (**17.3km**) – even though Matera is signed R! Around the corner, branch R on a lane, NW once more. Peace and quiet reign on this enjoyable undulating section. Waymarks don't abound here so check GPX tracks if in doubt.

Heading uphill, go N past a conifer wood, followed by olive groves and buildings. At a road (**21km**), go uphill then R under an **old railway arch**. When you gain a ridge, take a 90-degree turn L onto a minor road with promising views to rock caves and a canyon, heading NW towards the outskirts of a built-up area. But just when you think the day's enjoyment is about to end, the VE swerves R past flats to pick up a road R (SE) past a bikers' club and gated properties. At a corner (**22.5km**, **Dimore all'Ofra**), turn L for a lovely stretch N on a rock base through shrubs, close to the edge of a dramatic ravine.

At a field, bear L (NW) up past houses to tarmac, then out to busy **Via Cappuccini**. This leads R past houses, shops and bus stops then R again onto **Via Casalnuovo**. About 500m along, don't miss the fork R for the *Chiese rupestri* route. You're led out to the breathtaking edge of the canyon, with Matera spread out ahead of your amazed eyes. Follow the paved stepped way past rock dwellings, lookouts and cafés, taking your time. The VE bears L to Via Bruno Buozzi and down to the superb **belvedere** near the **church of San Pietro Caveoso**.

Take the street L past I Tre Portali into Rione Pianelle then swing L and R onto

The pale clay terrain surrounding Montescaglioso

stepped **Via Muro**, heading steeply uphill through the marvellous ancient town. At the top, a short way L sees you emerge into the surprisingly spacious piazza with the soaring Duomo (cathedral) of **Matera** (400m, **27km**) and the VE's rewarding conclusion. Finding your way around Matera is not a simple affair so allow plenty of time to locate your accommodation.

MATERA 🔺 ⬡ ⬡ 🍴 ⛪ 🏧 ➕ 🅗 ℹ️ ⬛ ◼️

LOCAL REP: ANTONIO, TEL 328 6481954
STAMP: STATIO PEREGRINORUM, VICO III CASALNUOVO (TESTIMONIUM TOO); LE LUCANE, VIA BECCHERIE 13

Volumes can be written about this unique rock town made up of labyrinthine *rione* (districts) known as the Sassi (stones), its buildings both below and above ground. Overlooking a dramatic canyon and spread over adjacent outcrops, Matera is punctuated with churches and belltowers, which make handy landmarks as orientation can be confusing to say the least. The word 'maze' does not do it justice.

Dozens of *chiese rupestri* (cave churches), many frescoed, dot the surrounds. A guided walk around town is highly recommended; make sure it includes the mammoth underground cistern known as the 'Palombaro lungo' beneath Piazza Vittorio Veneto.

A visit to the opposite side of the yawning canyon is a must. A low Himalayan-style bridge leads across the bottom, and good paths climb up the steep flanks exploring cave chapels, dwellings and plenty more. Naturally this is an excellent photo vantage point for Matera.

See the Introduction for more.

Matera – Via Ellenica

❶ B&B Fiorentini   ❷ B&B Mikasa   ❸ Hotel Albergo Roma   ❹ Ostello dei Sassi

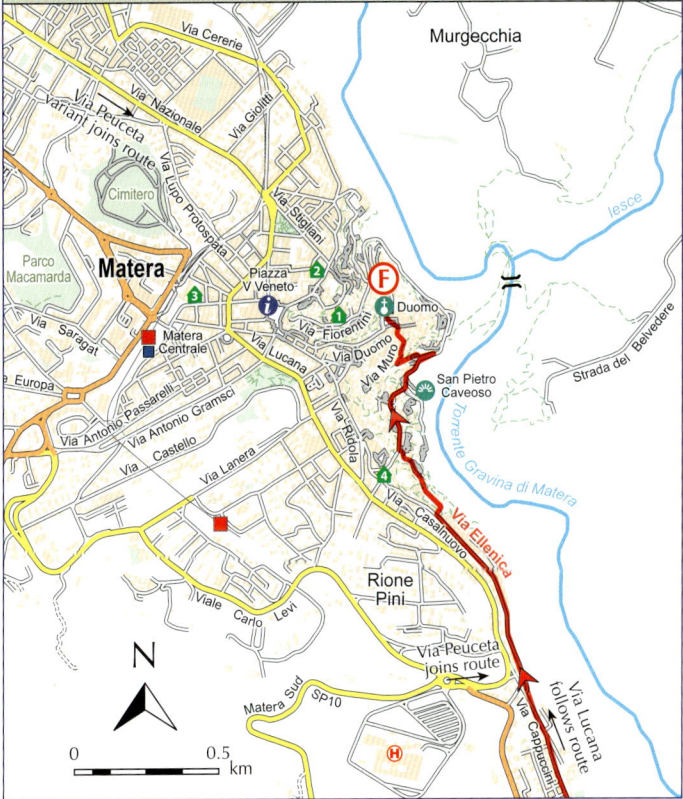

Follow the 'Chiese rupestri' sign into Matera

itinerario turistico

Circuito urbano delle Chiese Rupestri

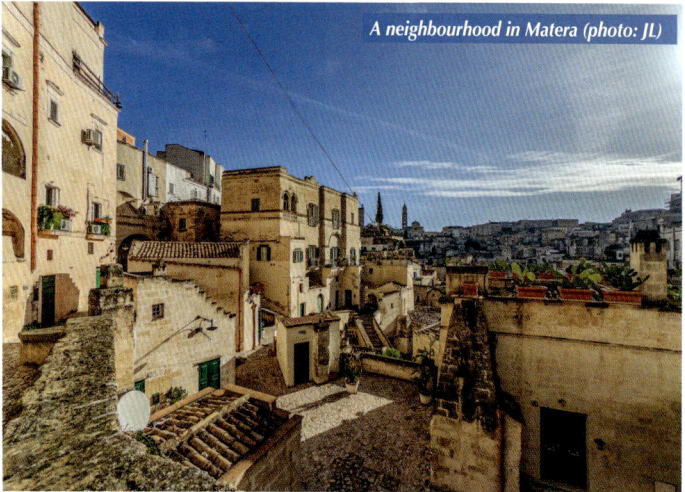

A neighbourhood in Matera (photo: JL)

VIA LUCANA

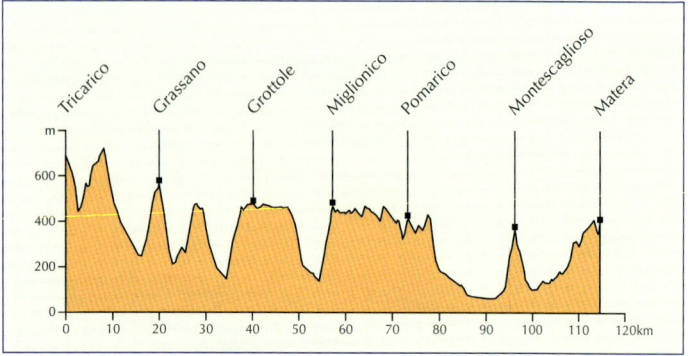

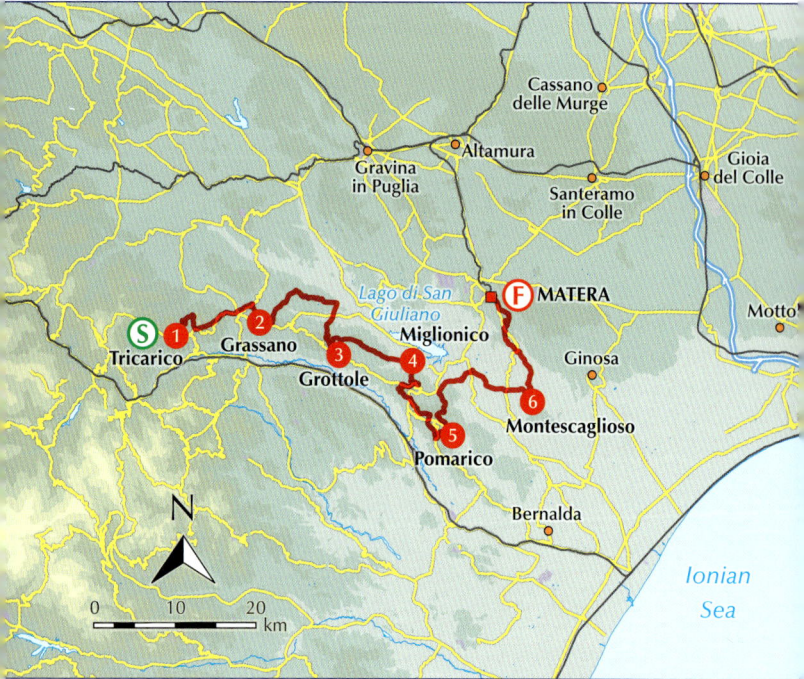

Start	Tricarico
Finish	Matera
Time	6 days (32hr 30min)
Distance	114.6km
Ascent	2930m
Descent	3205m
Getting to Tricarico	Sita (www.sitasudtrasporti.it) or Titobus (www.titobus. it/autolinee tel 0835 726017) from Matera (train or bus from Bari), otherwise train from Naples via Potenza to Grassano Scalo station. A shuttle bus runs up to town; otherwise ask your accommodation provider to pick you up.
Note	In the following description, the Via Lucana is abbreviated as VL.

Getting to the Cammino start

From the bus stop in Tricarico, walk N along Viale Regina Margherita past cafés and restaurants. Where the road forks near a park and school, go L in ascent to where the Torre Normanna stands (allow 5min).

TRICARICO ⬆ 🍴 🏛 ATM ➕ ▣

LOCAL REP: MARILENA, TEL 320 7013814
STAMP: KRISTIN'S CAFÈ, VIALE REGINA MARGHERITA 101

Probably named after the Greek for 'three hills', Tricarico has an especially colourful multicultural history, with a palace, castle and churches to match. Once a staging post on the Roman Via Appia, it boasts an Arab–Norman district with watchtowers, and was home to thriving Jewish and Albanian communities in the 15th–16th centuries. Intriguing carnival traditions dating back to pagan times feature battles between brightly costumed men dressed as cows and bulls.

A more recent 20th-century figure was young activist–mayor Rocco Scotellaro, author of *Peasants of the South*. He had a lane constructed to facilitate the peasants' access to their fields, even ensuring stones were incorporated to prevent the mules from slipping.

STAGE 1
Tricarico to Grassano

Start	Torre Normanna, Tricarico
Finish	Piazza Arcangelo Ilvento, Grassano
Time	5hr
Distance	20.5km
Total ascent	720m
Total descent	865m
Difficulty	Moderate
Percentage paved	50%

This straightforward although rather long opening stage sets out through the paved streets of medieval Tricarico before crossing undulating farming areas alternating with woods. There are lots of downs and ups. It concludes with a gentle climb through open fields to brilliantly placed Grassano, spread along a wind-blown ridge with vast views. Refreshments are available on a short detour a little after the halfway mark.

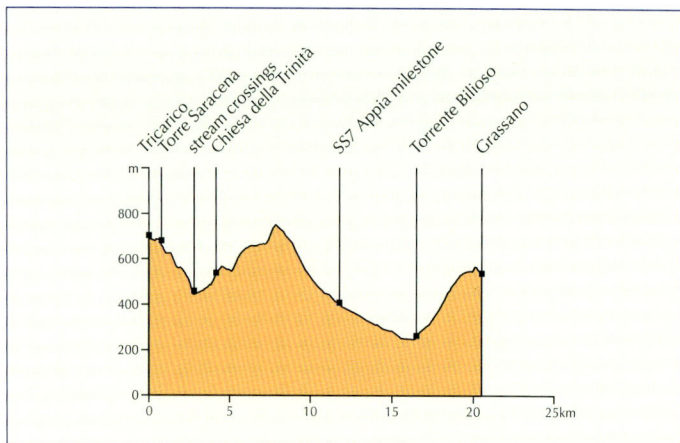

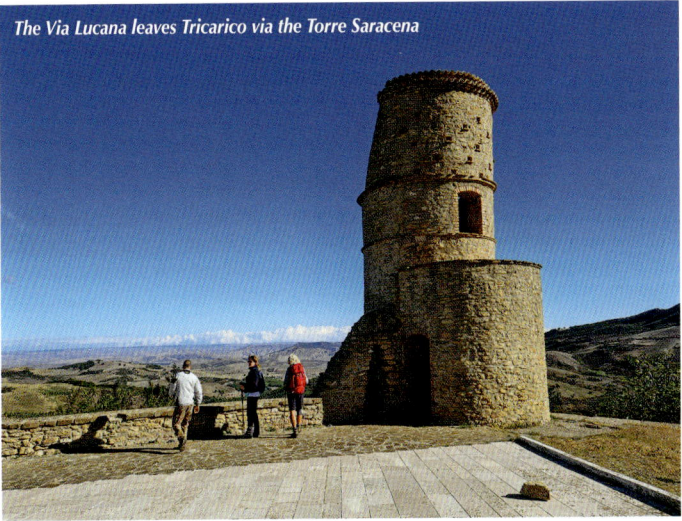

The Via Lucana leaves Tricarico via the Torre Saracena

The VL starts at the foot of the marvellous 27m-tall Torre Normanna in Tricarico (698m). The official route returns to the main road and continues NW via Piazza dell'Emigrante, with its mural of Rocco Scotellaro, and through to Piazza Garibaldi and its cafés. Alternatively, from the Torre Normanna, by all means take the slightly higher parallel way past Chiesa di San Francesco to Piazza Garibaldi. Now turn L across the square and through the paved streets of the old town past the Palazzo Ducale and the rear of the cathedral. Lined with palaces, Via Laura Battista concludes at the modest **Torre Saracena** (**1km**), a marvellous lookout over Valle del Bradano.

Well waymarked, a quiet road then a concreted lane descend a broad ridge lined with broom to a knoll, **Fronte Pizzuto** (**1.7km**), on the old way trodden by peasants. Zigzag down to **cross a stream** (**2.8km**) twice – take care after heavy rain. From a water treatment plant, a lane (soon surfaced) loops past a well-run council kennel for stray dogs (*rifugio canile*) and climbs to the atmospheric ruins of **Chiesa della Trinità** (**4.2km**). After rounding a hill, join a road S through rolling farmland past a drinking fountain. Here there are inspiring views to the so-called Dolomiti Lucane mountains.

Keep L at a busy road near a house (**7.4km**) then soon the VL goes L on a lane, passing a gas pipe, to climb steeply into oak woods on a sunken stretch. Over a rise past a gated property, a path takes over, dodging a ditch – watch your step.

After a **farm**, follow the edge of a field towards long sheds for a faint path R to cross the road (**10.1km**).

Proceed NE to a giant oak tree before the VL emerges at a roadside **milestone** (SS7 Appia) then cuts the next corner for 1.3km of tarmac due E, flanked by vast fields and lines of hills punctuated with wind turbines. A bit over halfway (**13km**), fork L for 'Pascale arredamenti' and a truck yard. Keep L across a minor road. (An 800m detour R leads to the café **Ristoro dell'Anno Santo**.)

A line of cypress trees leads to an **old well** and on through olive trees to a farm surrounded by eucalypts. A gentle descent sees you cross a stream near a derelict red building. Out at the road (**16km**), turn R towards a bridge over the **Torrente Bilioso**, but make sure you veer L before it for a lane and *metanodotto* (gas pipe) signs.

In the company of reeds and prickly pear, cross a **bridge** then start the final climb of the day, heading mostly SSE through wheat fields and olives then into shady oak woods. Further up, the lane is concreted through orchards. Up at buildings and a road, the VL veers L (ignore straight ahead for the *centro*) onto cobbled panoramic **Strada 'I Cinti'**. This runs below the village, past walls of layered compressed sand and rock dating back 1–2 million years, originally below sea level. Strada 'I Cinti' is home to cellars where snow was once stored and grapes are still pressed.

At a park, fork sharp R past what's left of the 15th-century castle (erected by the Knights of Malta), then up steps to the foot of the Chiesa Madre (cathedral). Keep L following waymarks to where the stage concludes in Piazza Arcangeli Ilvento in **Grassano** (526m, **20.5km**), with its white belltower, landmark fountain, Municipio and bus stop.

GRASSANO 🔵 🟠 🟢 ⓐ ⊕ ⬛

LOCAL REP: MICHELE, TEL 329 6663056
STAMP: CHIESA MADONNA DEL CARMINE, PIAZZA ILVENTO

Piazza Arcangeli Ilvento was named after a leading Italian specialist in infectious diseases who hailed from the village. Another great figure associated with Grassano was Carlo Levi, the Italian anti-fascist activist, writer and artist who was exiled here in 1935. In his landmark book *Christ Stopped at Eboli* (1945), he wrote: 'Grassano, like all the villages hereabouts, is a streak of white at the summit of a bare hill, a sort of miniature imaginary Jerusalem in the solitude of the desert. I liked to climb to the highest point of the village, to the wind-beaten church, where the eye can sweep over an endless expanse in every direction, identical in character all the way around the circle. It is like being on a sea of chalk, monotonous and without trees.'

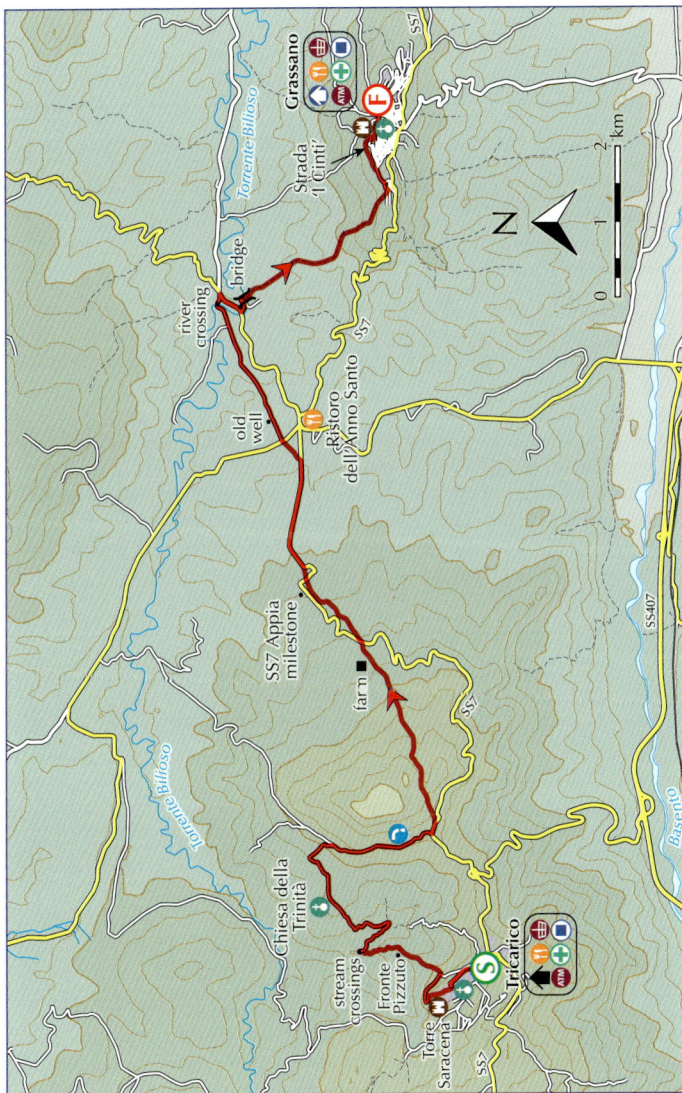

Grassano

Strada 'I Cinti'

Torrente Bilioso

bridge

river crossing

old well

Ristoro dell'Anno Santo

SS7 Appia milestone

farm

Torrente Bilioso

Chiesa della Trinità

stream crossings

Fronte Pizzuto

Torre Saracena

Tricarico

Basento

N

0   1   2 km

STAGE 2
Grassano to Grottole

Start	Piazza Arcangeli Ilvento, Grassano
Finish	Piazza Aldo Moro, Grottole
Time	6hr
Distance	19.8km
Total ascent	710m
Total descent	770m
Difficulty	Moderately hard
Percentage paved	50%

With long downhills and steep uphills, this memorable day has a rewarding central stretch along the broad Altojanni ridge with 360-degree views. After a superbly located monastery, you touch on ruins of a medieval settlement before recrossing the main valley via farms and fields. The stage does entail rather a lot of road walking but traffic is very light and you can walk on the grassy verge most of the time.

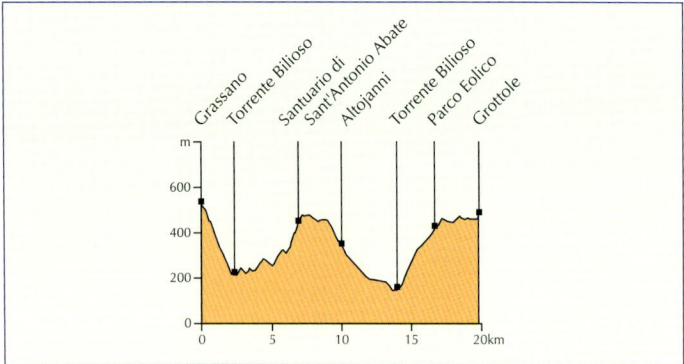

From Grassano's Piazza Arcangeli Ilvento, turn downhill N out of town on Via Tilea past playing fields. Where the road forks, keep L down the steep narrow way, passing an old drinking fountain (**0.5km**) dating back to 1879. A patchwork

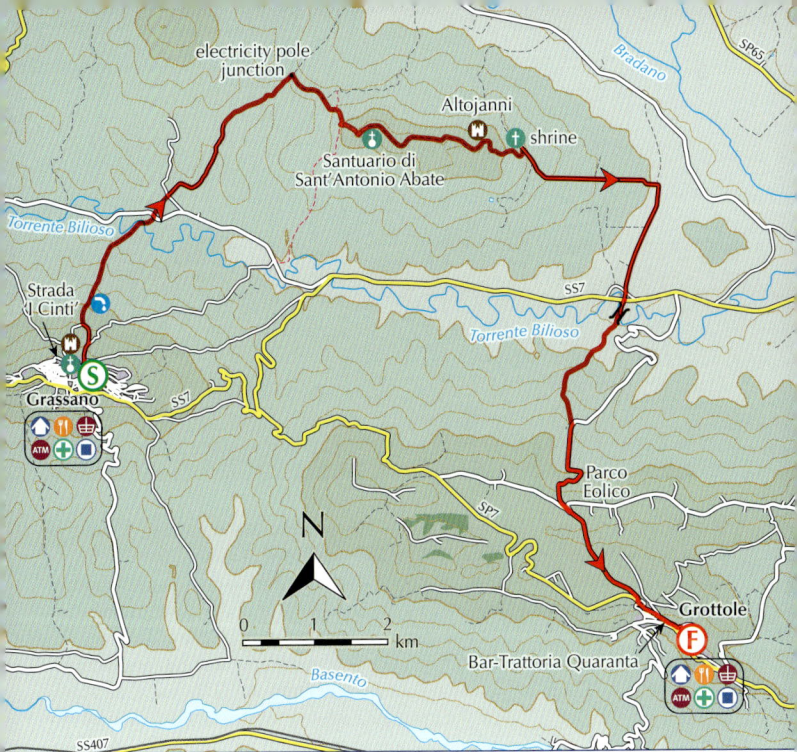

of fields and rural properties and myriad fruit trees accompany the descent, whIch finally concludes at a concrete bridge over **Torrente Bilioso**. Up at the **main road** (**2.5km**), cross straight over for a lane NE where the VL joins up with the red/white Sant'Antonio Abate route.

More relaxing now, the route proceeds gently uphill through fields and over rises, dipping across a series of small streams (muddy after rain). As the gradient steepens, don't miss a fork R past a clay outcrop. Up at a signposted **junction and electricity pole** (**5.5km**), branch R (SE) on a clear lane towards the foot of a hill surmounted by a building (Sant'Antonio Abate, where you're headed). A bumpy stone track – near vertical! – leads up through lentisc thickets, forking L to the brilliant wind-blown position of **Santuario di Sant'Antonio Abate** (568m, **7.2km**). Currently uninhabited, the hospice and church were built in 1371 to treat sufferers of leprosy and ergotism, which is known across Europe as 'St Anthony's fire'.

A good level lane carries on due E to a square tower (**9km**), a remnant of medieval **Altojanni**, followed by a gentle descent. Lago di San Giuliano appears ahead.

The Santuario di Sant'Antonio Abate in its wind-blown spot

At a **shrine**, you join a narrow tarmac road descending past properties. Finally, at a raised water pipe, veer R (SSW) to the **SS7 main road** (**13.7km**). The VL crosses straight over to pick up a lane and recross the **Torrente Bilioso** on a concrete bridge. Not far on, don't miss the fork L onto a path uphill into woodland alternating with fields. At a clear lane, go L to olive groves and out to a **road** (**15.9km**).

Stick with the road mostly S in ascent near giant wind turbines and through an intersection (**17km**) in the **Parco Eolico** (wind farm). A hollow excavated with grottoes precedes a rise, where the town of Grottole finally comes into sight. At the main road, turn L past houses and schools to the fork at welcoming Bar-Trattoria Quaranta, where a refreshing drink is the order of the day. Go L uphill to Piazza Aldo Moro in **Grottole** (481m, **19.8km**), where the stage officially concludes.

GROTTOLE ⬡ 🍴 🏛 🏧 ➕ ⬛
LOCAL REP: ILARIA, TEL 333 2724724
STAMP: BAR-TRATTORIA QUARANTA, VIA NAZIONALE 52; CHIESA SANTA MARIA MAGGIORE, LARGO PAPA GIOVANNI XXIII
The laid-back village occupies a high ridge above the Basento and Bradano valleys. Its history, stretching back to prehistoric then ancient Greek and Roman times, has left a maze of narrow paved one-way streets where talented residents squeeze their cars in. Don't miss the unusual *Chiesa diruta*, the skeleton of a church that was erected in the 16th century but was damaged by earthquakes and fell into disrepair.

Grottole was named after its numerous caves and grottoes; go and explore the rear of the settlement, whose rocky earth face is riddled with *cantine* (cellars) where wine presses still operate.

STAGE 3

Grottole to Miglionico

Start	Piazza Aldo Moro, Grottole
Finish	Castello, Miglionico
Time	5hr
Distance	17km
Total ascent	445m
Total descent	450m
Difficulty	Moderate
Percentage paved	30%

A pretty straightforward and very enjoyable stage, mostly spent walking along a broad ridge with a vast outlook, in the company of humming wind turbines for a while. The day's reward is delightful hilltop Miglionico, with an ornate church and an impressive visitable castle.

Leave Grottole from Piazza Aldo Moro the way you came in, downhill out of the old part of town to the fork at **Bar-Trattoria Quaranta**. Walk straight ahead along the main road then branch R on Via S Maria delle Grazie (signed for the *cimitero*). After a stream crossing, take a minor road L (ENE) through fields and over a rise to a rough path L dipping across the valley floor. Up on a concreted lane you gain a ridge with **wind turbines** and turn R on a lane (**2.2km**).

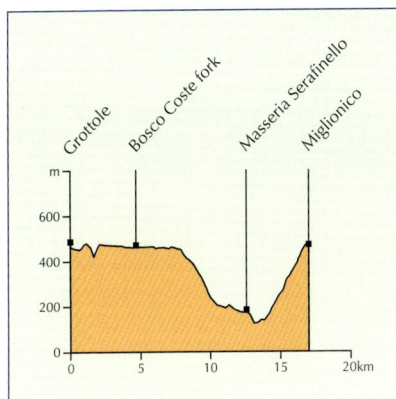

Easy level walking E is the flavour here, so you have time to enjoy the view back to Grottole and everywhere else. Ignore the **fork L** (**4.8km**) signed for Bosco Coste and continue on to cross a road (**6km**); Lago di San Giuliano comes into sight below. Ignore turnoffs. As the ridge begins to peter out, bid farewell to the wind turbines (**8.5km**) and start a winding descent through woodland and rolling wheat fields. Miglionico, your destination, appears on its distant ridge.

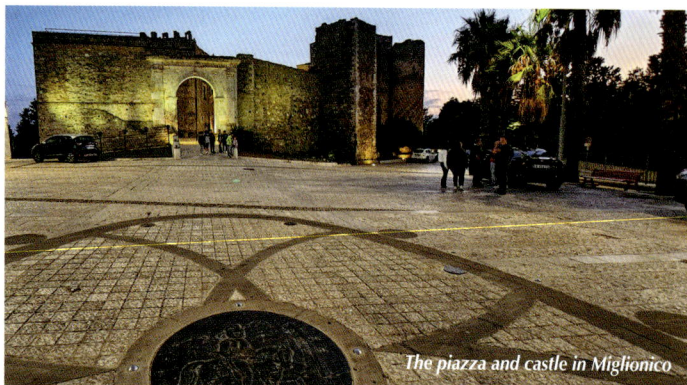

The piazza and castle in Miglionico

After a bridge near farms then a T-junction (**12.5km**) near **Masseria Serafinello**, a minor road heads R, due S past smallholdings to the valley floor. Now comes the final slog of the day in the company of sheep, olive groves and wild fruit trees. Stops to get your breath back are perfect opportunities to enjoy views of far-off Matera beyond the lake.

Up at a **roundabout** (**16.5km**) and petrol station, go L uphill into beautiful Miglionico. You quickly find yourself at the 14th-century Chiesa Madre, aka Basilica di Santa Maria Maggiore. Keep L through to Piazza del Popolo then R to the spacious square and stage conclusion at the Castello in **Miglionico** (465m, **17km**).

MIGLIONICO 🔺 ⬆ ⬆ 🍴 🏦 🏧 ➕ ℹ️ ⏹️

LOCAL REP: ANTONIO, TEL 328 6481954

STAMP: LAS MANAS CAFÈ, PIAZZA POPOLO 2; LA BOTTEGA DEI PIACERI, VIA PAPA GIOVANNI XXIII; PRO LOCO, CASTELLO DEL MALCONSIGLIO

Rightfully recognised as one of the *Borghi più belli d'Italia* (Italy's most beautiful villages) Miglionico is set on a high ridge between the Bradano and Basento river valleys. Its chequered history stretches back to at least the 6th century BC, when it was founded as a fortified military colony. As happened in this region, it was taken over by the ancient Greeks, Sunnites, Romans, Turks…each of whom left their style.

The marvellous 8th–9th-century Castello del Malconsiglio (www. castellodelmalconsiglio.it) is open to visitors; it was the site of a dramatic 1485 conspiracy by barons of the Kingdom of Naples against King Ferdinand I of Aragon, explained convincingly in a multimedia exhibition. Lastly, do find time for the Chiesa Madre, which boasts 18 exquisite 1499 oil panels painted by Cima di Conegliano.

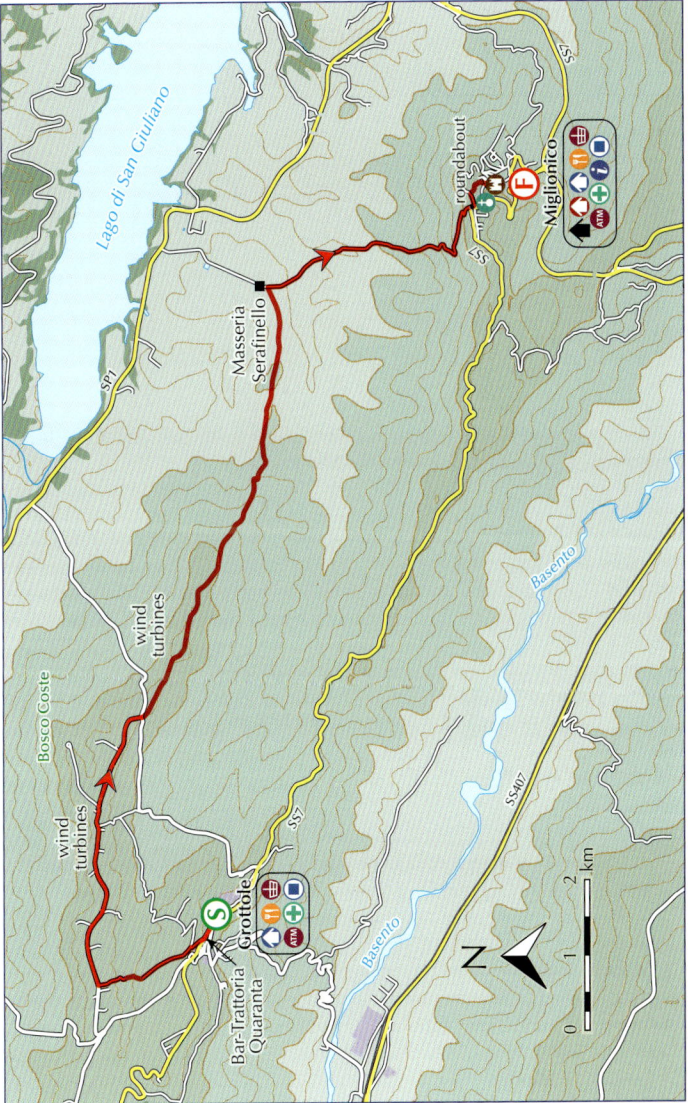

Lago di San Giuliano

Miglionico

roundabout

SS7

Masseria
Serafinello

SP1

SS7

SS7

SS407

Basento

wind
turbines

Bosco Coste

wind
turbines

Grottole

Bar-Trattoria
Quaranta

Basento

N

0   1   2 km

143

STAGE 4
Miglionico to Pomarico

Start	Castello, Miglionico
Finish	Palazzo Marchesale, Pomarico
Time	4hr 30min
Distance	16km
Total ascent	215m
Total descent	255m
Difficulty	Easy–moderate
Percentage paved	30%

This is a leisurely stage through rural areas and shady oak woodland then open countryside as it approaches fascinating Pomarico.

Facing the Castello at Miglionico, turn R down the road past a park and on to the roundabout and petrol station where you entered the town on the previous stage. Turn L up Via Papa Giovanni XXIII (bakery) and continue past the **cemetery** (**0.7km**). You're quickly out in the countryside, and you go L past a water tower. Soon it's R onto a gloriously scenic lane past a fig plantation. At houses, keep straight ahead through woodland to the **SS7 road** (**3km**).

Take the road opposite signed for Pomarico, looking over the Basento valley. Fork L onto an undulating gravel lane SE in the company of rock roses. The Pollino mountain range can be admired due S. A faint fork L leads to the hermitage **Madonna della Porticella** (**5.5km**) in a clearing with an ancient oak tree and picnic tables.

> The chapel of **Madonna della Porticella** (meaning 'little door') was named after a statue that appeared in a doorway to a young shepherd who, together with his flock, took refuge from a storm here.

From the oak tree, keep L to resume the lane (Carraia Porticella), with rosemary bushes and an **antenna** (**6km**) then shady oak woods. A rough track signed for Pomarico forks R (**7km**). If the track is fenced off for livestock, ensure you close it after you. Due E now, a leisurely, level stretch reaches ponds, picnic tables and drinking water (**8km**).

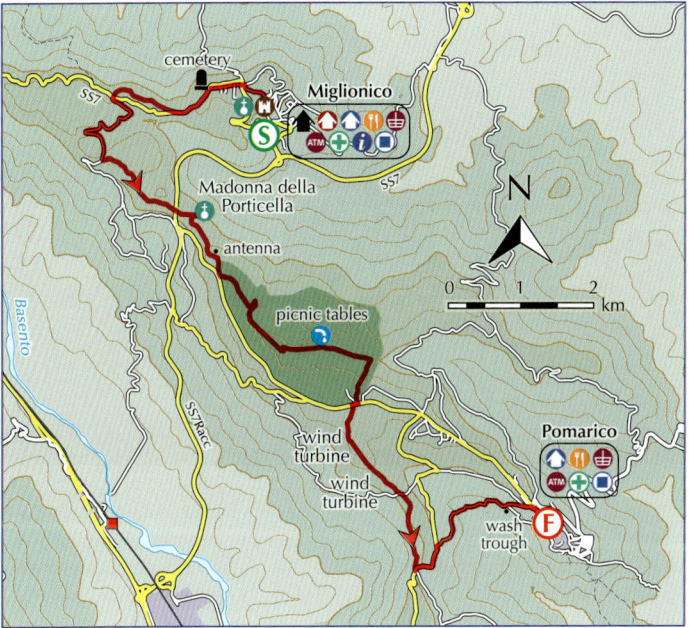

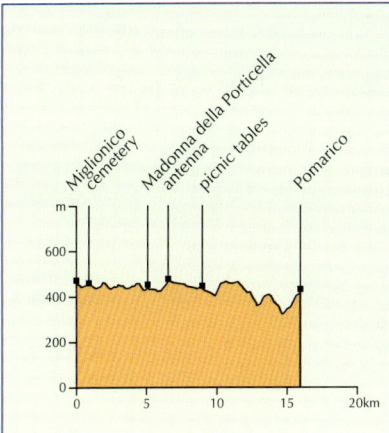

The VL proceeds through woodland to a main road (**9.5km**). Go R then L up to a **wind turbine**. As the lane becomes stony, bear L past solar panels – Pomarico comes into view E. Follow the ridge past another turbine to a house (Villa Armandi) and cross a minor road. A lane proceeds past olive trees and grapevines to join another road (**13km**) before a narrow shady road branches R (NE) downhill, passing houses with lion statues on guard.

The landmark oak tree at Madonna della Porticella

Among eroded clay terrain, a bridge crosses a stream before an old **wash trough** to gain a main road. Turn R for the final metres past the cafés lining Corso Giuseppe Garibaldi into **Pomarico** (459m). The stage concludes at the imposing square building Palazzo Marchesale (**16km**), home to the town's historical archives.

POMARICO ⬡ 🍴 🚲 ＡＴＭ ✚ ◼

LOCAL REP: GIANNI, TEL 389 8381332
STAMP: BAR CENTRALE, CORSO GARIBALDI 10; CAFFÈ MARCHESALE, PALAZZO MARCHESALE

Pomarico has lots of surprises in store. The fascinating high part of the village has remarkably steep narrow streets flanked by stone walls draped with caper vines. All-round views sweep over the predominantly clay and sand terrain, which erodes easily, threatening buildings and forming ridges known as *calanchi*.

Pomarico was the birthplace of Camillo Calicchio, a tailor who travelled north to Venice to work for the doges who ruled the city; believe it or not, he was the grandfather of the great Venetian composer Antonio Vivaldi! A Vivaldi music festival is held here every year to honour him.

The village name derives from 'land of apples'. Culinary specialities here include fragrant *porcelli* buns flavoured with wild fennel, and *scarcella*, focaccia filled with egg, sausage and scamorza cheese.

The pretty, narrow streets of upper Pomarico

STAGE 5

Pomarico to Montescaglioso

Start	Palazzo Marchesale, Pomarico
Finish	Piazza del Popolo, Montescaglioso
Time	6hr 30min
Distance	22.8km
Total ascent	405m
Total descent	470m
Difficulty	Moderately hard
Percentage paved	60%

Although this stage is rather long, it is both rewarding and varied. The central section has a lot of walking on roads, albeit quiet and minor, and you can make the most of the grassy verges. The entry into Montescaglioso is simply wonderful.

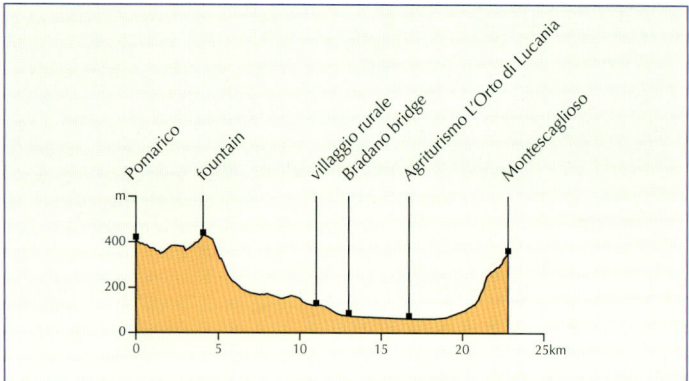

In Pomarico, walk through the Palazzo Marchesale building, with its bakery and café. Out the other side, go L then R down steps flanking an imposing former convent. Keep L past a bright yellow house then take the road signed 'tutte le direzioni'. Not far downhill, go L alongside a portico for the gentle descent in

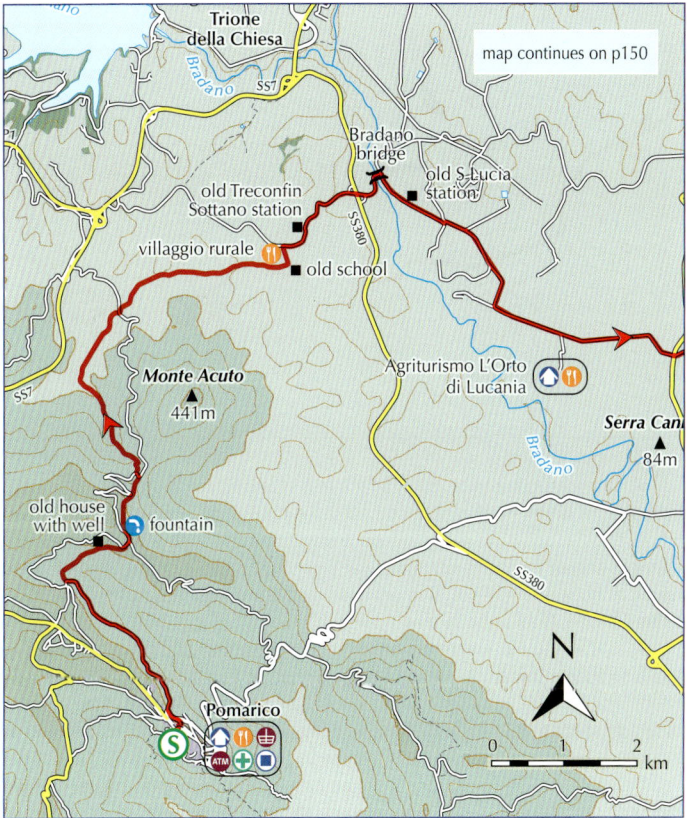

map continues on p150

the company of broom bushes followed by oak woods with farms. A waymarked lane breaks off (**3km**) in descent, soon overgrown as it crosses a stream bed with conifers before heading up NE to a clearer lane and olive trees then an **old house with a well**. This was once a staging post on an ancient 'motorway' trade route.

Up at a road, it's not far to a **fountain** (**4.2km**, drinking water). A shady lane N offers lovely views to Lago San Giuliano and Monte Acuto straight ahead, not to mention Montescaglioso an awfully long way off E. A descent due N plunges through a field to emerge on the roadside a tad uphill of a ruined shed. In wet weather, by all means take the road to the L in lieu of the field.

VL waymarks point you down a lane into *calanchi* (eroded terrain) then open land. After a R fork, walk through to a disused railway line, and continue on past a house, olive trees and rolling wheat fields. On a rise with a derelict building, a former **school** for the nearby post-war settlement, keep L through the **villaggio rurale** to houses where you can get water and refreshments (last shed on the L, **11km**). You're about halfway now!

Turn R to the old **Treconfini Sottano railway station** and follow the road to a flyover then a **bridge** over the deep canyon of the **Bradano River**. Immediately afterwards go R (SE) on a lane past the old **Santa Lucia railway station**, then on past farm sheds to join a road R flanking a raised concrete aqueduct. Ahead on its hill stands Montescaglioso, but it never seems to get any closer!

Fields of corn and vegetables see you pass ↻ **Agriturismo L'Orto di Lucania** (**16.7km**, refreshments) before a main road (**18.5km**), where you cross onto a lane lined with eucalypts. The inevitable climb awaits. And yes, it's steep and possibly slippery in the wet due to the clay underfoot. You puff up to shady tree cover and a fountain (not drinkable) then follow the main road uphill. At picnic tables by all means shortcut the corner up to an intersection (**22km**) at the foot of a knoll with a Madonna statue.

Take the minor road L winding uphill past houses. As Via Montevetere it approaches the town's rear flank – don't miss the fork R for a rough steep track up via caves and wine cellars, enjoying amazing views. Steps lead through the arch of Porta Sant'Angelo into elegant Piazza del Popolo with its Benedictine abbey in **Montescaglioso** (352m, **22.8km**).

MONTESCAGLIOSO ⬡ 🍴 🏨 🏧 ➕ ❶ ⬛

LOCAL REP: LEONARDO, TEL 388 8971972
STAMP: IL BARLUME, CORSO REPUBBLICA 92/94; DISPENSA CUCIBOCCA, CORSO REPUBBLICA 85

The name came from the ancient settlement called Mons Caveosus, its medieval nucleus dug into the rocky outcrop. The prosperous-looking town spreads gently along a ridge, its main street paved with gleaming white stone, narrow side alleys turning off at right angles. Several piazzas boast stately churches.

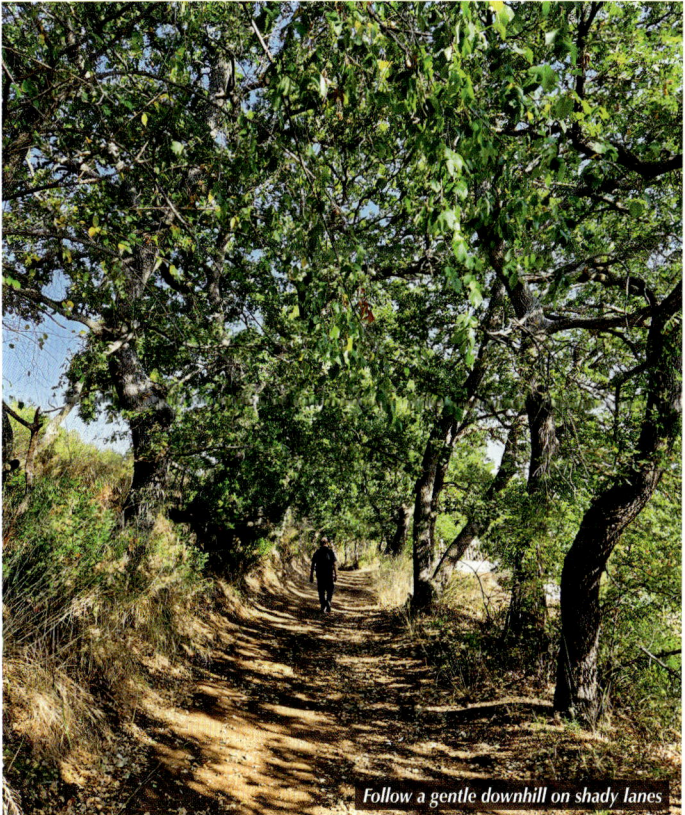

Follow a gentle downhill on shady lanes

STAGE 6

Montescaglioso to Matera

Start	Piazza del Popolo, Montescaglioso
Finish	Duomo, Matera
Time	5hr 30min
Distance	18.5km
Total ascent	435m
Total descent	395m
Difficulty	Moderate
Percentage paved	55%

Today's opening section is not brilliant as it takes a rather busy road, but then things improve with an enjoyable countryside traverse before the wonderful conclusion at spectacular Matera.

Should you prefer, there are direct buses from Montescaglioso to Matera; however – and this is a big however – it will mean missing the special entry to Matera.

Get yourself back to Piazza del Popolo in Montescaglioso and retrace your steps from Stage 5 through Porta Sant'Angelo. Don't miss the fork R down to Via Montevetere. If you reach a lookout with a 'megaphone', you need to backtrack. The road winds down to the intersection (**0.8km**) below a Madonna statue which you passed on Stage 5. Take the main road R and shortcut through trees to the picnic tables.

Continue down the rather busy road to a signed lane R (**2km**) that drops under a raised **pipeline** – then go sharp L through eucalypts back to the tarmac. After a hairpin bend comes a long straight stretch N (watch out for traffic). Keep straight ahead through two

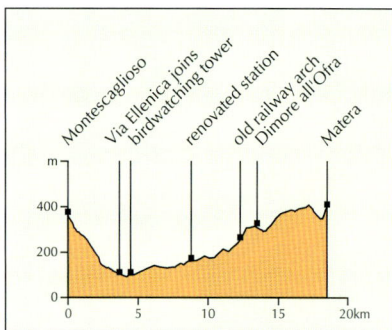

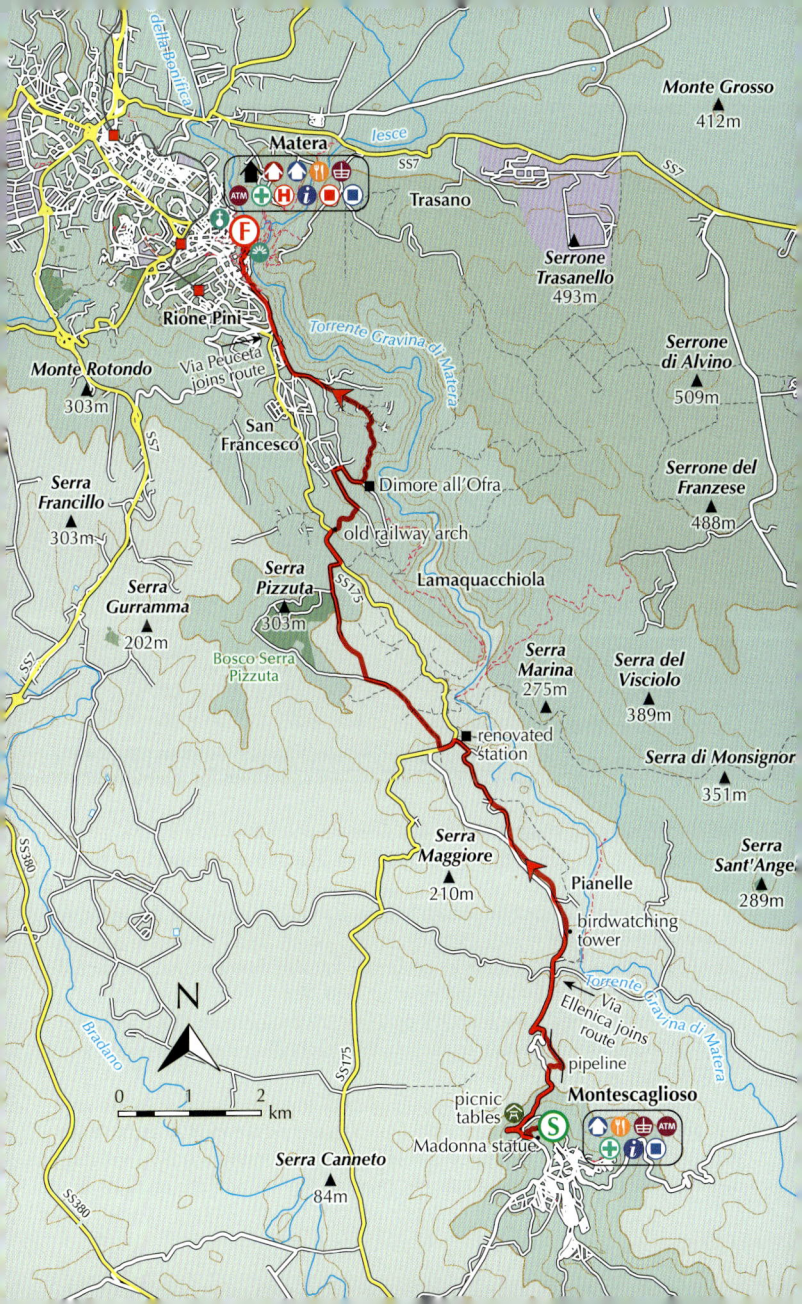

Matera

Trasano

Monte Grosso
412m

Serrone
Trasanello
493m

Serrone
di Alvino
509m

Serrone del
Franzese
488m

Rione Pini

Monte Rotondo
303m

Via Peuceta
joins route

San
Francesco

Torrente Gravina di Matera

Dimore all'Ofra

old railway arch

Lamaquacchiola

Serra
Francillo
303m

Serra
Pizzuta
303m

SS7

Bosco Serra
Pizzuta

Serra
Gurramma
202m

Serra
Marina
275m

Serra del
Visciolo
389m

Serra di Monsignor
351m

renovated
station

Serra
Maggiore
210m

Pianelle

Serra
Sant'Ange
289m

birdwatching
tower

Bradano

Via
Ellenica joins
route

Torrente Gravina di Matera

pipeline

picnic
tables

Montescaglioso

Madonna statue

Serra Canneto
84m

N

0   1   2
|————————|————————|
                    km

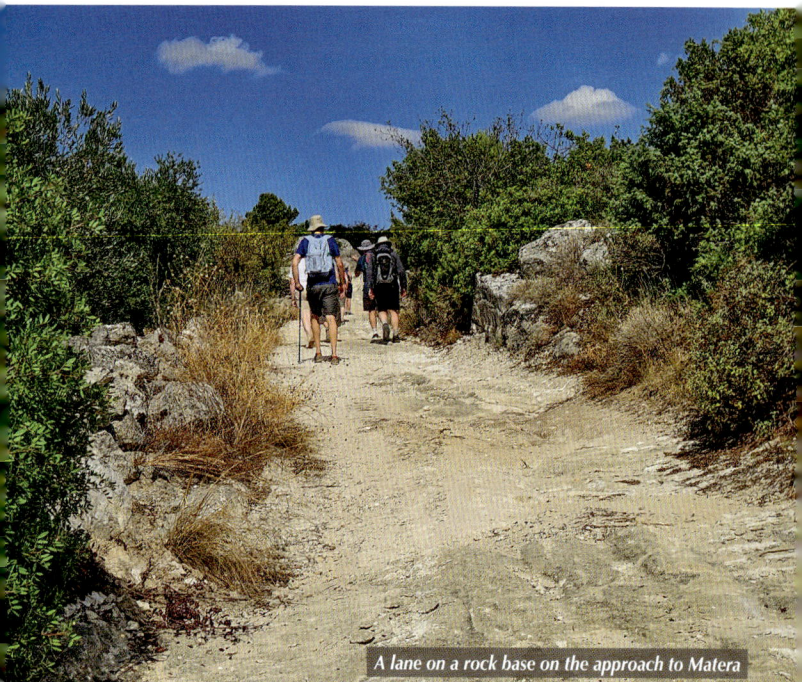

A lane on a rock base on the approach to Matera

intersections (in common with the Via Ellenica now) then take the faint lane breaking off R. Parallel to the road, it passes a quarry and **birdwatching tower** (**4.2km**).

The ensuing long straight stretch follows a former railway line through tiny farms and the **Pianelle** *centro visite*, becoming a cycle track. Where the old railway is overgrown, the VL continues on tarmac towards vineyards. At a **renovated station building**, turn L along the main road (**8.3km**) – even though Matera is signed R! Around the corner, branch R on a lane, NW once more. Peace and quiet reign on this enjoyable undulating section. Waymarks don't abound here so check GPX tracks if in doubt.

Heading uphill, go N past a conifer wood, followed by olive groves and buildings. At a road (**12km**), go uphill then R under an **old railway arch**. When you gain a ridge, take a 90-degree turn (**13km**) L onto a minor road with promising views to rock caves and a canyon, heading NW towards the outskirts of a

San Pietro Caveoso and its piazza in Matera

built-up area. But just when you think the day's enjoyment is about to end, the VL swerves R past flats to pick up a road R (SE) past a bikers' club and gated properties. At a corner (**13.5km**, wind turbine), turn L for a lovely stretch N on a rock base through shrubs close to the edge of a dramatic ravine.

At a field, bear L (NW) up past houses to tarmac, then out to busy **Via Cappuccini**. This leads R past houses, shops and bus stops then R again onto **Via Casalnuovo**. About 500m along, don't miss the fork R for the *Chiese rupestri* route. You're led out to the breathtaking edge of the canyon, with Matera spread out ahead of your amazed eyes. Follow the paved stepped way past rock dwellings, lookouts and cafés, taking your time. The VL bears L to Via Bruno Buozzi and down to the superb **belvedere** near the **church of San Pietro Caveoso**.

Take the street L past I Tre Portali into Rione Pianelle then swing L and R onto stepped **Via Muro**, heading steeply uphill through the marvellous ancient town. At the top, a short way L sees you emerge into the surprisingly spacious piazza

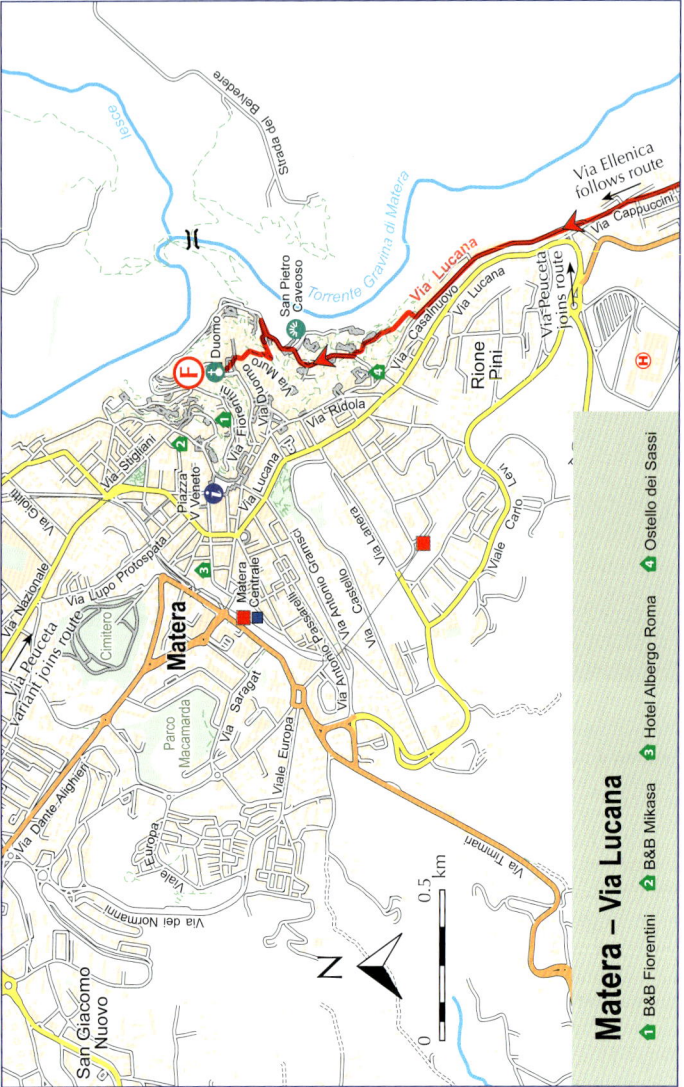

Matera – Via Lucana

1 B&B Fiorentini   2 B&B Mikasa   3 Hotel Albergo Roma   4 Ostello dei Sassi

with the soaring Duomo (cathedral) of **Matera** (400m, **18.5km**) and the VL's satisfying conclusion. Finding your way around Matera is not a simple affair so allow
plenty of time to locate your accommodation.

MATERA ⛺ ◑ ◐ 🅗 🏧 ⊕ 🅗 ⓘ ◉ ◉

LOCAL REP: ANTONIO, TEL 328 6481954
**STAMP: STATIO PEREGRINORUM, VICO III CASALNUOVO (TESTIMONIUM TOO); LE
LUCANE, VIA BECCHERIE 13**

Volumes can be written about this unique rock town made up of labyrinthine
rione (districts) known as the Sassi (stones), its buildings both below and above
ground. Overlooking a dramatic canyon and spread over adjacent outcrops,
Matera is punctuated with churches and belltowers, which make handy landmarks as orientation can be confusing to say the least. The word 'maze' does not
do it justice.

Dozens of *chiese rupestri* (cave churches), many frescoed, dot the surrounds.
A guided walk around town is highly recommended; make sure it includes the
mammoth underground cistern known as the 'Palombaro lungo' beneath Piazza
Vittorio Veneto.

A visit to the opposite side of the yawning canyon is a must. A low
Himalayan-style bridge leads across the bottom, and good paths climb up the
steep flanks exploring cave chapels, dwellings and plenty more. Naturally this is
an excellent photo vantage point for Matera.

See the Introduction for more.

APPENDIX A

Accommodation

The international dialling code for Italy is 39. If calling an Italian landline, include the initial zero, regardless of whether you're calling from inside or outside Italy. Mobile phone numbers begin with 3.

Stage	Location	Name	Type	Facilities
ALL ROUTES				
	Matera	Ostello dei Sassi	▲	Sleeps 50 in dorms + rooms
		B&B Fiorentini	◔	Sleeps 7
		Albergo Roma	◔	Sleeps 20
		Mikasa	◔	Sleeps 6
VIA PEUCETA				
1	Bari	Habari We Dorm Hostel	▲	Sleeps 12
		L'Ape che Gira	◔	Sleeps 2
1	Bitetto	Casa Ester	▲	Sleeps 6
		B&B dei Nobili	◔	Sleeps 20
		La Maison da Francy	◔	Sleeps 7
2	Cassano delle Murge	B&B Le Dimore del Garibaldi	◔	Sleeps 20
		Ca' Felice	▲	Sleeps 4
		Country Pub Pecora Nera	◔	Sleeps 18
3		Agriturismo Battista	◔	Sleeps 6
3		Agriturismo Amicizia	◔	Sleeps 40
3		Masseria Galietti	▲	Sleeps 10 in dorm

⬆ Hostel   🔴 hotel   🔵 B&B

	Tel	Web/email	Comments
	0835 312586	lostellodeisassi@gmail.com	Kitchen
	329 3639640	www.bebfiorentini.com	
	0835 333912	https://albergoroma-matera.it	Handy for the railway station
	388 0761914	mikasa.mt@virgilio.it	
	080 8170525	www.habarihostel.com	
	334 9614423	lapechegira@gmail.com	
	340 6051347	lestera1972@gmail.com	Run by cammino rep. Donation. Dinner possible
	334 3673960	hotel.deinobili@virgilio.it	Dinner possible
	351 7509838	lamaisondafrancy@gmail.com	
	347 6415278	www.dimoredelgaribaldi.it	
	388 6074723		Run by cammino rep
	080 3072088	www.pecoranerapub.it	1.2km SW out of town; restaurant. Home to Sant'Euligio, CM patron saint (see Introduction)
	080 3327107	www.tenutabattista.com	
	080 763393	www.agriturismoamicizia.it	
	338 8376461	giaccheverdisanteramo@gmail.com	3km before Santeramo. Self-catering

Stage	Location	Name	Type	Facilities
3	Santeramo in Colle	B&B L'Incontro	○	Sleeps 15
		Hotel Volante	○	
		Ostello Mamre	▲	Sleeps 106
4	Altamura	Antico Castello	○	
		Casa Xenia	○	*Sleeps 10*
		Martini Home 11	○	Sleeps 8
5	Gravina in Puglia	B&B Duca Orsini	○	Sleeps 16
		La Tana della Volpe	▲	Sleeps 6
6		*Masseria Santa Maria*	○	*Sleeps 16 in rooms + dorms*
6	Santuario di Picciano	*Masseria La Fiorita*	▲ ○	*Sleeps 45 in dorms + rooms*
VIA ELLENICA				
1	Brindisi	Hotel Barsotti	○	Sleeps 100
		B&B Mare Nostrum	○	Sleeps 10
		B&B Dionisio	○	Sleeps 4
1	San Vito dei Normanni	B&B Quadrifoglio	○	Sleeps 8
2	Carovigno	Bed & Bread Piazza 'Nzegna	○	Sleeps 12
		B&B Coppularossa	○	Sleeps 9
3		*B&B La Vigna*	○	*Sleeps 12*
3	Ostuni	Hotel Centro Spiritualità Madonna della Nova	○ ▲	Sleeps 96 in rooms + dorms
		I 7 Archi	○	Sleeps 19

Tel	Web/email	Comments
333 4026202 338 7876011	incontro1992@gmail.com	
080 8173718	https://volantehotel.com	
393 8917729	www.mamre.biz	
368 7877859		
328 9254928	giovannifratusco1966@gmail.com	Run by cammino reps
345 0157294	bebmartini044@gmail.com	
080 3224322 339 7943945	www.ducaorsini.it	Run by cammino rep
380 7676235	latanadellavolpe50@gmail.com	Run by cammino rep
334 6067028	*fcasareale@libero.it*	*3.5km from route. Pickup and drop-off included. Dinner available*
327 7084471 *335 7224180*	*masserialafiorita@gmail.com*	*7km from the Santuario. Transport to and from included. Dinner available*
347 2187683	www.hotelbarsotti.com	
329 2375705	bandbmarenostrum@libero.it	
349 6750870		
340 7470696	www.ilquadrifogliodeinormanni.it	
327 4023097	www.bbpiazzanzegna.com	
340 6963329	bebcoppularossa@gmail.com	
333 2258756	www.bblavigna.com	*5.5km beyond Carovigno, 15km before Ostuni*
368 580055 331 9331699	madonna.pellegrina@libero.it	1.5km E out of town. Dinner available
340 7678217	www.i7archi.com	

Stage	Location	Name	Type	Facilities
4	Cisternino	La Casa dei Nonni	⬭	Sleeps 9
		B&B La Casetta	⬭	Sleeps 3
5	Locorotondo	B&B Due Cuori e una Casetta	⬭	Sleeps 2
		B&B Trulli Manuela	⬭	Sleeps 8
6	*Coreggia*	*B&B 5 Lune*	⬭	*Sleeps 4*
6	Alberobello	Hotel Silva	⬭	Sleeps 30
		Hotel Airone	⬭	Sleeps 45
7	Martina Franca	MOROLAin	⬭	Sleeps 5
		B&B Ciao Bello	⬭	Sleeps 9
8		*Foresteria Bosco delle Pianelle*	⬥	*Sleeps 12*
8	Crispiano	B&B Paisà	⬭	Sleeps 6
		B&B Del Corso	⬭	Sleeps 4
9		Masseria Amastuola	⬭	Sleeps 36
9	Massáfra	B&B Sotto La Volta	⬭	Sleeps 16
		B&B Casa Camilla	⬭	Sleeps 9
		B&B Corte Laterza	⬭	Sleeps 7
10	Mottola	Albergo Diffuso Vecchia Mottola	⬭	Sleeps 50
		B&B La Dimora di Maria	⬭	Sleeps 3
11	Castellaneta	Japp'e Japp'e	⬥	Sleeps 10, dorm + room
		B&B Sedile Quattro	⬭	Sleeps 4
		B&B Nova Domus	⬭	Sleeps 10

Tel	Web/email	Comments
339 8708066	famigliamoggia@alice.it	
347 5187303		
334 2350030		
334 8937209	trullimanuelavacanze@gmail.com	
329 3048373		
392 2037016	www.hotel-silva.it	
080 4322804		
327 0113025	morolainitalia@gmail.com	
320 4887250	bebciaobello@gmail.com	
080 4400950 *348 3526958*		*22km beyond Martina Franca, 5.4km before Crispiano. Donation. Self-catering*
389 4263289	paisabeb@gmail.com	
328 3772736	egse2002@libero.it	
099 9908025	www.amastuola.it	
339 3603823	info@sottolavolta.it	
350 1631111	info@casacamilla.eu	
333 9606169	cortelaterza@gmail.com	Kitchen
376 1598296	vecchiamottola@gmail.com	Run by cammino rep. Rooms in different parts of town
340 2300417	nikocaramia@yahoo.com	No breakfast
333 1052345	ostellomariapugliese@yahoo.com	Run by cammino reps
388 8513347	sedilequattro@gmail.com	
329 7490370	novadomus2014@gmail.com	

Stage	Location	Name	Type	Facilities
12	Laterza	B&B Iris	⟳	Sleeps 12 in dorm + rooms
		La Ferula	⟳	Sleeps 4
13	Ginosa	B&B Corte Fiorita	⟳	Sleeps 9
		Dimora di San Martino hostel	▲	Sleeps 15 in dorm + room
VIA LUCANA				
1	Tricarico	Feni House	⟳	Sleeps 12
1	Grassano	La Casa del Belvedere	⟳	Sleeps 6
2	Grottole	Dimora Chiesa Diruta	⟳	Sleeps 4
		Il Nido delle Rondine	⟳	Sleeps 10
		Terrazzo sul Basento	⟳	
3	Miglionico	Il Belvedere Appartamento	⟳	
		Hostel Lupus in Fabula	▲	Sleeps 6 in dorm
		Il Ritrovo del Cima	⟳	*Sleeps 12*
4	Pomarico	Alle Porte di San Rocco	⟳	
		Casa Zia Nunziatina	⟳	
5		Agriturismo L'Orto di Lucania	⟳	Sleeps 20
5	Montescaglioso	B&B La Volta	⟳	
		Il Borgo Ritrovato (Albergo diffuso)	⟳	Sleeps 20
		Foresteria dell'Abbazia	⟳	Sleeps 8

Tel	Web/email	Comments
348 2315005	www.irisbedandbreakfast.com	Run by cammino rep
329 8278085	nadia.giannico@gmail.com	Run by cammino rep. Laundry facilities
327 9559479	enrica.destena2016@gmail.com	
388 8971972	dimorasanmartino.ginosa@gmail.com	Run by cammino rep
338 7427320	www.fenihome.it	
328 4645542		Kitchen
334 9579277		Kitchen
349 7743247	www.ilnidodellerondini.com	Located just before the village
320 3680000		Outside village centre
348 2940930		Kitchen
328 6481954		Run by cammino rep. Kitchen, no breakfast
0835 559918	*www.ilritrovodelcima.it*	*3km south of town*
328 7778325		
328 6584727		
333 9802592	www.ortodilucania.it	6.1km before Montescaglioso. Restaurant
331 9097058		
388 9383073	https://ilborgoritrovato.com/index.php/en/hotel-in-montescaglioso-matera	Rooms around town
331 2388929	www.foresteriabbazia.com	

APPENDIX B
Italian–English glossary

Italian	English
abbazia	abbey
albergo	hotel
albergo diffuso	hotel with rooms around town
alimentari	groceries
bancomat	ATM
basilica	cathedral
belvedere	lookout, viewpoint
biglietto andata/ritorno	one-way/return ticket
bosco	woodland
calanchi	eroded clay terrain with gullies
camera	bedroom
cammino (plural: cammini)	long-distance walking route
cantina	cellar, usually for wine storage
casina	large house
castello	castle
cattedrale	cathedral
cava	quarry
cena	dinner
centro storico	old part of town
centro visite	visitor centre
chiesa	church
chiesa ipogea, chiesa rupestre	cave church
chiesa madre	cathedral
ciclovia	cycle track
colazione	breakfast

Italian	English
conto	bill, check
contrada	neighbourhood, town district
duomo	cathedral
fermata di autobus	bus stop
focacceria	focaccia bakery
foresteria	hostel
frantoio	olive press
gravina (plural: gravine)	ravine, canyon shaped by flowing water
lama	shallow canyon
masseria (plural: masserie)	large old-style farm building
municipio	town hall
panetteria, panificio	bakery
parco eolico	wind farm
pineta	pine wood
pista ciclabile	cycle track
pista pedonale	walkers' track
pranzo	lunch
pro loco	tourist information
rione	neighbourhood, town district
riserva naturale	nature reserve
sotterraneo	underground
stazione ferroviaria	railway station
sterrata	lane, unsurfaced road
supermercato	supermarket
tenuta	estate
treno	train
trullo (plural: trulli)	traditional cone-roofed hut in Puglia
via (plural: vie)	way, road, street

APPENDIX C
Useful contacts

Tourist information offices

Alberobello
Via Monte Nero 1
tel 379 2987173
www.prolocoalberobello.it

Altamura
Piazza Repubblica 11
tel 080 3143930
www.viaggiareinpuglia.it/en/
dettaglio-localita/altamura

Bari
Piazza dei Ferraresi 29
tel 080 5242244
www.bariexperience.com

Brindisi
Via Duomo 20
tel 0831 229784
www.visitbrindisi.it

Carovigno
Corso Emanuele 25
tel 393 0834404

Cassano delle Murge
Via Miani 11
tel 080 3211608 or 339 3959879

Castellaneta
Via Roma 112/114
tel 327 0576528

Ginosa
Via San Giovanni
tel 328 4852250
www.visitginosa.com

Gravina in Puglia
Piazza Benedetto XIII
tel 080 2043321
www.gravinainmurgia.com

Laterza
Palazzo Marchesale
Piazza Plebiscito
tel 099 8296793
www.laterzaturismo.com

Locorotondo
Via Morelli 24
tel 080 4312788

Martina Franca
Piazza XX Settembre 3
tel 080 4116554

Massafra
Piazza Garibaldi
tel 099 8804695
www.massafraturismo.it

Matera
Via Cappelluti 34
tel 0835 336572
www.materaturismo.it

Miglionico
Piazza Castello
tel 329 1221445

Montescaglioso
Piazza S Giovanni Battista
tel 0835 200630

Mottola
Viale Jonio/Via Lucania
tel 099 8867640
www.mottolaturismo.it

Ostuni
Corso Mazzini 8
tel 0831 1982471
www.ostunithewhitecity.com

Santeramo in Colle
Piazza Garibaldi
tel 331 9971701

San Vito dei Normanni
Piazza Leonardo Leo
tel 0831 955 236
www.comune.sanvitodeinormanni.br.it

Cammino Materano

General: https://camminomaterano.it

Accommodation: https://camminomaterano.it/strutture-ricettive

Public transport

Trains
FAL: https://ferrovieappulolucane.it/en
Trenitalia: www.trenitalia.com

Buses
Flixbus: www.flixbus.it
Sita: www.sitasudtrasporti.it
Titobus: www.titobus.it/autolinee
STP: www.stpbrindisi.it

NOTES

NOTES

DOWNLOAD THE GPX FILES

All the routes in this guide are available for download from:

www.cicerone.co.uk/1260/GPX

as standard format GPX files. You should be able to load them into most online GPX systems and mobile devices, whether GPS or smartphone. You may need to convert the file into your preferred format using a conversion programme such as gpsvisualizer.com or one of the many other such websites and programmes.

When you follow this link, you will be asked for your email address and where you purchased the guidebook, and have the option to subscribe to the Cicerone e-newsletter.

CICERONE

www.cicerone.co.uk

LISTING OF CICERONE GUIDES

BRITISH ISLES CHALLENGES, COLLECTIONS AND ACTIVITIES

Great Walks on the England Coast Path
Map and Compass
The Big Rounds
The Book of the Bivvy
The Book of the Bothy
The Mountains of England and Wales:
  Vol 1 Wales
  Vol 2 England
The National Trails
Walking the End to End Trail
Cycling Land's End to John o' Groats

SHORT WALKS SERIES

15 Short Walks Hadrian's Wall
15 Short Walks in the Lake District:
  Keswick, Borrowdale and
  Buttermere
15 Short Walks in the Lake District:
  Windermere Ambleside and
  Grasmere
15 Short Walks Lake District:
  Coniston and Langdale
15 Short Walks in Arnside and
  Silverdale
15 Short Walks in the Ribble Valley
15 Short Walks in Nidderdale
15 Short Walks in Northumberland:
  Wooler, Rothbury, Alnwick and
  the coast
15 Short Walks in the Yorkshire
  Dales: Grassington, Skipton,
  Malham and Ilkley
15 Short Walks in the Peak District:
  Bakewell and the White Peak
15 Short Walks on the Malvern Hills
15 Short Walks in Cornwall:
  Falmouth and the Lizard
15 Short Walks in Cornwall: Land's
  End and Penzance
15 Short Walks in the South Downs:
  Brighton, Eastbourne and Arundel
15 Short Walks in the Surrey Hills
15 Short Walks on Dartmoor North:
  Okehampton and Chagford
15 Short Walks on Dartmoor South:
  Ivybridge and Princetown
15 Short Walks on Exmoor
15 Short Walks Winchester
15 Short Walks in Bannau
  Brycheiniog: Brecon Beacons
15 Short Walks in Pembrokeshire:
  Tenby and the south
15 Short Walks in Dumfries and
  Galloway
15 Short Walks in the Trossachs:
  Callander and Aberfoyle
15 Short Walks on the Isle of Mull
15 Short Walks on the Orkney Islands
15 Short Walks on the Shetland
  Islands

SCOTLAND

Ben Nevis and Glen Coe
Cycling in the Hebrides
Cycling the North Coast 500
Great Mountain Days in Scotland
Mountain Biking in Southern and
  Central Scotland
Mountain Biking in West and North
  West Scotland
Not the West Highland Way: A
  Mountain High Way
Scotland
Scotland's Best Small Mountains
Scotland's Mountain Ridges
Scottish Wild Country Backpacking
Skye's Cuillin Ridge Traverse
The Borders Abbeys Way
The Great Glen Way
The Great Glen Way Map Booklet
The Hebridean Way
The Hebrides
The Isle of Mull
The Isle of Skye
The Skye Trail
The Southern Upland Way
The West Highland Way
The West Highland Way Map Booklet
Walking Ben Lawers, Rannoch
  and Atholl
Walking in the Cairngorms
Walking in the Pentland Hills
Walking in the Scottish Borders
Walking in the Southern Uplands
Walking in Torridon, Fisherfield,
  Fannichs and An Teallach
Walking Loch Lomond and the
  Trossachs
Walking on Arran
Walking on Harris and Lewis
Walking on Jura, Islay and Colonsay
Walking on Mull, Coll and Tiree
Walking on Rum and the Small Isles
Walking on the Orkney and Shetland
  Isles
Walking on Uist and Barra
Walking the Cape Wrath Trail
Walking the Corbetts
  Vol 1 South of the Great Glen
  Vol 2 North of the Great Glen
Walking the Fife Pilgrim Way
Walking the Galloway Hills
Walking the John o' Groats Trail
Walking the Munros
  Vol 1 Southern, Central and
  Western Highlands
  Vol 2 Northern Highlands and the
  Cairngorms
Winter Climbs in the Cairngorms
Winter Climbs: Ben Nevis and
  Glen Coe

NORTHERN ENGLAND ROUTES

Cycling the Reivers Route
Cycling the Way of the Roses
Hadrian's Cycleway
Hadrian's Wall Path
Hadrian's Wall Path Map Booklet
The Coast to Coast Cycle Route
The Coast to Coast Map Booklet
The Coast to Coast Walk
Walking the Dales Way
The Dales Way Map Booklet
Walking the Pennine Way
Pennine Way Map Booklet

LAKE DISTRICT

Bikepacking in the Lake District
Cycling in the Lake District
Great Mountain Days in the Lake
  District
Joss Naylor's Lakes, Meres and
  Waters of the Lake District
Lake District Winter Climbs
Lake District:
  High Level and Fell Walks
  Low Level and Lake Walks
Mountain Biking in the Lake District
Outdoor Adventures with Children
  — Lake District
Scrambles in the Lake District —
  North
  South
Trail and Fell Running in the Lake
  District
Walking The Cumbria Way
Walking the Lake District Fells —
  Borrowdale
  Buttermere
  Coniston
  Keswick
  Langdale
  Mardale and the Far East
  Patterdale
  Wasdale
Walking the Tour of the Lake District

NORTH-WEST ENGLAND AND THE ISLE OF MAN

Cycling the Pennine Bridleway
Isle of Man Coastal Path
The Lancashire Cycleway
The Lune Valley and Howgills
Walking in Cumbria's Eden Valley
Walking in Lancashire
Walking in the Forest of Bowland
  and Pendle
Walking on the Isle of Man
Walking on the West Pennine Moors
Walking the Ribble Way
Walks in Silverdale and Arnside

For full information on all our
guides, books and eBooks,
visit our website:
www.cicerone.co.uk